T0197097

Crumbs for a Hungry Soul

Bibb Underwood

authorHOUSE®

AuthorHouse™
1663 Liberty Drive
Bloomington, IN 47403
www.authorhouse.com
Phone: 1 (800) 839-8640

Published by AuthorHouse 02/22/2018

ISBN: 978-1-5462-2579-9 (sc)
ISBN: 978-1-5462-2580-5 (hc)
ISBN: 978-1-5462-2578-2 (e)

Library of Congress Control Number: 2018900947

Print information available on the last page.

Any people depicted in stock imagery provided by Thinkstock are models, and such images are being used for illustrative purposes only. Certain stock imagery © Thinkstock.

This book is printed on acid-free paper.

Because of the dynamic nature of the Internet, any web addresses or links contained in this book may have changed since publication and may no longer be valid. The views expressed in this work are solely those of the author and do not necessarily reflect the views of the publisher, and the publisher hereby disclaims any responsibility for them.

Contents

VI. Crumbs Dropped on My Friend's Back Porch

VII. Old and Sometimes Stale Crumbs

VIII. Crumbs from a Smart Alec's Mouth

Foreword

Crumbs for a Hungry Soul is NOT a religious book. It came out of a desire to capture permanently some brain droppings that were manifested over a period of time. I'm not sure what really motivated all this. Perhaps, it is the dregs of curiosity that drove me to see if I could write a coherent sentence on a subject of interest to someone besides myself. Perhaps it was the need to vindicate my high school English teacher. Perhaps it was just pure vanity.

Whatever it was, it all began by accident. I met a woman working in a mental health center who seemed to be so dedicated to the mentally handicapped people with whom she worked, I sat down and got her story. Then I wrapped it in my impression of her. I took it to the San Marcos Daily Record and asked them to run it because I was so impressed with Donna Schoonover that I wanted others to meet her, if only vicariously.

The Neighbors Editor at the time, Linda Keese, read it and her reaction was, "How many of these can you write?" From a complete lack of experience, I blurted out, "One a week." So, began the weekly ritual of staring at a blank page and questioning my sanity.. That led me to produce my first book, **Ordinary People, Heroes, Creators and Survivors,** some 200 plus profiles for the Record and in the process, these extra Crumbs made their way to the paper.

To say that I have enjoyed writing these pieces and the construction of the poems might be a stretch. It can be said without fear of contradiction, however, that I have deeply enjoyed having written. There is some sarcasm, some wisdom, and, I hope, some humor, contained herein. So, I have published this volume to share with you, in a permanent format, the fruits of my labors—labors of love, I might add.

My greatest reward will be your enjoyment and appreciation of the book.

Bibb Underwood

Introduction

This book is a deep sampling of my experience, history, thoughts, and ideas, all gleaned from a rural childhood, followed by four years at Texas A&M and 27 years as an Infantry officer. Following a satisfying and reasonably successful military career, I made a drastic change of professional pursuits and became a family therapist for some 20 years. What's between these pages is also between my ears and deep in my heart. As you read these essays and poems, my hope is that you will be able to say, "I know this person."

There was a time when I referred to my writing as "navel-gazing," and dismissed it as an idle pursuit on a level with solving crossword puzzles. On a personal dare, I sent a few of my scribblings to the local newspaper, The San Marcos Daily Record, and from the feedback I received, concluded that, perhaps these essays deserved more respect than I gave them.

To protect and preserve these thoughts, I have put almost 100 of them in this book with the hope that others in more scattered and varied places may be attracted to this literary effort. It will make an ideal book to place next to the TP. Each essay, in general, is less than a thousand words. If nothing else, it will fill an otherwise idle time.

There is no theme in the book, or maybe there are several themes in the book. It covers childhood adventures and misadventures; it deals with politics and prejudices; it contains some light-hearted pieces; it contains some reviews, some histories, and some reflections. Some of the pieces and poems are written with sarcasm; some to share a bit of wisdom; some contain some humor. Scattered, serendipitously, throughout are poems. The book reflects some of my emotions; it makes statements; it is, simply put, a part of *my* soul.

Occasionally, I re-read these essays and the poetry and I find it touches me much more deeply now than it did when I wrote. As I read and reflect it, I find myself in a better mood, I'm strengthened and fulfilled. I'm no longer searching and pondering and questioning.

So, **Crumbs for the Hungry Soul** is what I find in these pages. I hope you do.

Bibb Underwood

Grunts

They were collectively known as Grunts, a Viet Nam era word that so perfectly described the lot of the men to whom it referred, it gained universal usage. No green berets, no silver wings, no fancy flight suits. They wore sweat stained fatigues draped from shoulder to ankle like a wrinkled green crust. Their head and face were enveloped in a steel pot with a camouflage cover on which was often written some reminder of a different world, a different time. A girlfriend's or a wife's name might be prominently displayed. A DEROS (Date Estimated to Return from Overseas) date might be indelibly etched in a prominent place. Frequently, the following was boldly copied: *Yea, though I walk through the valley of the shadow of death, I fear no evil, for I am the meanest mother.... in the valley.* Some had pocket-sized New Testaments stuck in the elastic camouflage band. Each of them had his own way of dealing with the internal fear that was always present.

"Grunt" was a name which, initially, conjured up disdain or stupidity or extremely bad luck. Over time, tenacity and bravery turned it into a name worn with pride—to the point that many claimed it without earning the right to it. Officially, Grunts were combat infantrymen of the United States Army and Marines. They were drafted off a farm in Iowa; they were African American with an Alabama drawl; they had an Italian name and grew up in New Jersey; they were raised in dire poverty on the reservations of New Mexico; they were just out of college and joined the service before embarking on a professional career; they heard only Spanish spoken in their home in the barrios of San Antonio until they went to first grade; they had dropped out of college and joined up to avoid the draft.

They were on the edge of their future. They were all together and engaged in an endeavor not fully understood. Nobody ever

1

fully understands war. But they were there. Come together in a most unlikely way. Doing things undreamed of months, weeks or even days earlier. They were there to do a job. A dirty job. A job many of their generation shirked. And they did it. They did it well. They did it at a great sacrifice to themselves and to their loved ones. They were unique. No one who does not experience it can ever know the true meaning of soldiering together in combat. In fact, 35 to 40 years later they are just *now* realizing the full meaning and depth of what they did for their country. And for each other.

In combat there is a bonding that develops as in no other circumstance. I don't know if it is love, faith, trust, or some unnamed feeling. But it is permanent. It can not be destroyed by time or pre-occupation. It is as permanent as the color of your eyes. This feeling grows deeper and stronger with time. Today, many of those Grunts will be remembering a fallen comrade. One who stepped on a land mine while walking point; one who took a sniper's bullet right through the name tag on his jungle fatigues. They will recall with extreme clarity the color of the sun that day, the exact sound of the first crack of the rifle. They will recall exactly what they were thinking just before the gut-wrenching explosion.

They were young, a little angry, perhaps. For sure, a little crazy, for they all thought they were bulletproof. But they were smart, energetic, well trained and, for the most part, well led. Life had not yet marked them and defined them. It was all in front of them, but at the moment, they were giving a part of that life to their country because they had been asked to do so. Without hesitation, without question, maybe with some doubt, certainly with some fear, they answered the call to serve. They found themselves with a rifle, a rucksack, a steel pot, a canteen of water, and a box of C-rations in the middle of a jungle facing God knows what, just twenty meters away. They were, as has always been the case, the point, the first, out in front; all others were there because the Grunts were there. The enemy's first shot was aimed at them. *They* had to dismantle the booby traps. *They* went into the tunnels, not knowing if a rifle or a pistol was pointed directly toward the path they were taking. *They* were first into the tree line. *They*

discovered it was a hot [enemy controlled] landing zone. They spent days of absolute tedium, punctuated by moments of pure terror.

They had the best supporting arms the world has ever known. The Grunts were supported by artillery that could shoot 17 miles. There were airplanes that could deliver tons of bombs on pinpoint targets in just minutes. They had the best radios available. Their weapons were specially designed for them. Helicopters could jerk a Grunt out of the jungle and fly him to a hospital miles away. But the single most important thing they had to keep them going–where they placed their greatest trust, that which mattered most, the ultimate reassurance–was each other.

As soldiers who answered the call and did their duty they deserve our deepest love and admiration. The Grunts must know in their mind that they have responded to the highest calling. They have served their fellow man. They put themselves in mortal danger for a cause and for another human. Many made the ultimate sacrifice. The majority of the names on the Wall in Washington, D.C. are the names of Grunts. But those who survived owe no apologies. They sacrificed time that can not be recalled. They gave everything they were asked to give. It is they who truly understand the meaning of life because they have faced death.

And when they did get back to the world, they once again showed their character and loyalty. Contrary to the popular myths, they did not return to this country as drugged out, traumatized mental wrecks. They were not constantly suffering flashbacks of unspeakable atrocities. They returned and in spite of the degradation and rejection heaped on them by those who did not serve, they wove themselves back into the fabric of the country as plumbers, carpenters, lawyers, doctors, priests, and retailers. They are socially responsible, concerned, productive citizens. Today, I hope you will take a few minutes and remember not only those who fell in all our wars, but say a prayer for the Grunt who today is in Germany, Korea, Afghanistan, and other far-flung military posts around the world in the interest of peace and prosperity for the rest of us.

The Grave

My body fell at Bunker Hill, at Concord and Lexington
Again in 1812 at Washington and Bladensburg
At Shiloh, Vicksburg, Gettysburg and Manassas
I stood in harm's way

I have a white marker in the Agonne
And at Chateau-Thierry and on the banks of the Marne
We lie in rows at Normandy, Luzon, Iwo Jima and North Africa
At peace today, our last vision was war

At Pusan, Inchon and Pork Chop Hill
I stood with comrades until I fell
And the cold of winter froze my corpse
I never asked why

I was at Khe Sahn, Ia Drang, and the Mekong
And now my name appears on a long
Slab of black granite
It is one of Fifty-Eight Thousand Two Hundred Thirty-Five

I fell in Bosnia, Serbia
And places you never heard of
In Iraq I felt the sting of desert sand twice
And knew again the ultimate sacrifice

Do you remember me
My name is Jones, O'Neal, Hernandez, Cloud, and Stein
I answered every call to duty with honor
And now my monument is the grave

It was not for glory that I served
Duty called
I gave it all
Pause today and remember

May 31, 2003
Memorial Day

Fear O' Faucet

When it comes to home repair, no matter how large or how small, I would rather French kiss a rattlesnake. You must understand, I am not totally without mechanical acumen. It is that I seem not to have the mind-set required to patiently assess the engineering principles involved in the construction and functioning of the simplest mechanical item commonly found in the home.

I have been known to convulse uncontrollably at the suggestion that there were curtain rods to be hung. I have left the county when faced with the task of removing and cleaning the AC filter. Replacing plugs and points of my automobile is equivalent to brain surgery in my hierarchy of difficult things to do. In short, you won't find me hanging out at your hardware store, auto parts place or a plumbing supply house.

It isn't that I can't do these things. Once I read some sage who said it was not a matter of skill, but a matter of time that kept us from becoming accomplished in these simple functions of life. How true. As mentioned earlier, I have little aptitude for scoping out the functioning and relationship of various parts of a given mechanical entity. My approach is the trial and error method. This requires a great deal of time. By the time I have discovered three ways to put it together, none of which work, it is time for dinner and the 23 parts of the toaster oven are occupying all available space on the kitchen counter. And I need to make one more trip to the parts store.

Imagine my consternation, then, when last week the kitchen faucet could no longer be coaxed into not leaking. I have spent the last three months playing an interesting game with the faucet. I position the handle in such a way that it appears to be off. I watch it as you would watch a willful child. Is it really going to do what you told it to do? Thirty seconds of watching and no leak. Ah, it is off. Turn, walk away and you hear ker-plop. It leaks. That was tolerable until the ker-plop became a steady stream. Out of respect for the rules for water use in our town, I decided I must fix the faucet.

This is no ordinary faucet. It produces hot and cold from a single spout and is controlled with a handle which closely resembles the steering mechanism of an F-16 fighter jet. I'm going to fix the faucet? Well, why not, I've got all day. Applying experience from previous adventures of this type, I did my usual study and preparation for the task at hand. Which means, as I walked out the door, I shouted to my wife, "What brand is that thing?" She told me.

If I go to the hardware store looking for a piece of aluminum pipe about this long, the clerk says, "Would that be half-inch or three-quarters?" and I immediately realize I don't have a clue. I stutter that it could be one or the other, and turn red while I try to bluff my way out of this idiotic predicament. Usually the clerk is astute enough to interrogate the truth out of me. "What you want it for? Oh, that takes a three-quarter, unless you got one of them Japanese models and that takes a 12 millimeter." At which point I'm sure I have the Japanese model. And they don't have the pipe. You get the picture.

Anyway, after wending my way through the garden hose, paint thinner, T-joints, and pink flamingos at the hardware store, I found faucet parts. Yea verily, I found little packets containing the "ball and stem"; packets containing the "seat and springs"; packets containing the "O Rings" (this is not the space shuttle is it?); and a packet containing all of the above, amen. The decision now is how many to get. I almost always manage to break the first one—or lose the essential lock washer, or hex nut, or ratchet spring. It is only a 10 minute drive to the hardware store. I'll take <u>one</u> complete packet and return if necessary. I fully expect to return.

Back home I approach the faucet as if stalking a full grown wolverine protecting its young. Fortunately, the packet had complete directions for replacing every part contained therein, even the "O" rings. After three sorties into the complexities of the faucet—the springs and seats were upside down once. And once I failed to turn the main cold water pipe back on (of course, I took the faucet apart again before I discovered that little omission)–the faucet was back in its original form and miracle of miracles, it worked!

You say your ice-maker is clogging up. Want me to take a look at it?

Going to the Grocery Store

For most people going to the grocery store is somewhere up there with a trip to the dentist, the gastroenterologist, or a visit from an IRS auditor. I like going to the grocery store.

The produce section is especially appealing to me. Viewing the bins of colorful fruit and vegetables is like walking into an art museum. The bright red tomatoes are displayed next to the deep green peppers. The sunshine yellow lemons lie next to the vividly colored oranges. Yellow squash and green squash contrast and complement to create a pallet of comfort colors. The spray has freshened the carrots, green beans, and parsley. The real marvel is that I know I can get tomatoes, squash or green beans in January. Or I can get an apple in August. What miracles are performed to have these products available to us all the time?

Walking the aisles and observing the endless number of products available is always mind-boggling. Talk about having choices! Once I have allowed my mind to close around the boundless inventory, it is immediately assaulted by the realization that almost all of those products can be purchased fresh, frozen or canned—in 12, 16, or 24-ounce sizes. And there are at least three brands of each item from which to choose. The grocery store is a place of wonder. It illustrates the abundance with which this country has been blessed, but even more, it illustrates the ability to harvest it, process it, distribute it, and make it available at prices most of us can easily afford.

I enjoy seeing my neighbors and friends who are tending their basic needs at the market. With some, it means a short conversation to catch up on the latest child or grandchild story. With some, I discover their illness has passed—or worsened. With others, I know there are issues far deeper than their basic needs. Often they will allow those issues to escape from the corners of their mind and expose them to light by sharing with a friend while pondering a light bulb purchase. Others choose to allow those burdens to lie in the dark, covered with the cloth of fear or denial.

The ancient Greeks used the term 'agora' to describe the market place. It literally means 'meeting place.' The grocery store fits the Greek definition. It is our agora.

The grocery store is where I see all sorts of people who live in this town. We all have to go to the store. There is the working mother, whose wrinkled forehead broadcasts the stress of her day, dashing in to grab a quick and easy meal for dinner. There is the young mother of two, balancing the needs of the family against the money available while explaining to her three year-old why he can't have three different boxes of his favorite cereal with the prizes inside.

At the end of the day, the concrete worker stops off to get a six-pack and a few other essentials to get him through the night. His clothes are covered with the dust of his labor; his shirt bears the outline of the day's sweat and he has the smell of work, reminding us we are all creatures of nature.

I enjoy the surprise of seeing someone long absent from my world. I enjoy seeing those I see more frequently, but I really enjoy seeing the checker who seems never to take a day off. It is reassuring to know that the young woman who is bagging my groceries is a biology major with only two semesters until graduation.

I enjoy seeing the experienced employee who offers advice about specials or recipes. Her overall appearance tells a story of a hard scrabble life. Her ruddy skin has not been softened with expensive lotion, her nail polish is chipped and forms erratic patterns, her hair color fits no well-defined description, and her hair knows only a vague familiarity with a comb and brush. She wears too tight jeans and a faded shirt. But her radiant smile erases those minor dings and dents and reflects the delight she takes in her work.

To fully appreciate the grocery store, one should spend time in a country where 'fresh chicken' means it is still wearing feathers—and cackling energetically. The choice of vegetables is beets, turnips and potatoes in the fall and tomatoes, squash and corn in the spring. Meat is exposed to whatever insect is disposed to take a sample of it. Your vendor most likely grew the product you wish to buy and his price will change depending on the appearance of your clothes or the fluency with which you speak his language.

Need milk? I'm going to the grocery store.

Retirement

Tuesday, January 25, the Austin American-Statesman carried William Safire's column on the op-ed page. I'm not a great Safire fan. Our politics are somewhat divergent, but I read his column whenever it appears. An old military adage is "Know your enemy," and while I do not consider him an enemy, I often thought of him as an adversary. You need to know them too. In Tuesday's column, he announced he was retiring from column writing. He will continue to write his column on language: usage, definitions, etc. I enjoy that when I can find it, in spite of his haughty tone and esoteric style.

He went on at some length, probably 1,000 words to explain that he was not retiring, but that he was changing his focus. He will become Chairman of the Dana Foundation, a group whose functions apparently are many, but their main activities include debating neuroethics and studying the effects of art, music, drama, etc. on later learning ability.

At 75, Safire is changing jobs and that was really what the Tuesday column was all about. He was elated that he would be giving up old routines to learn new skills. He would have to redirect and stimulate his brain. It would keep him youthful and vibrant.

It is not unusual today to compare the 60 year-old with the 50 year-old of yore. So, while retirement from our day job remains generally in the 60 to 65 year range, it is no longer accepted that the retiree will take his hard-earned security, retreat to the La-Z-Boy and vegetate while watching re-runs of Mayberry RFD. Exploring new pursuits and fresh stimulation of the brain and the body are what provides us with real Social Security in the retirement years.

The secret to laying aside the necessary resources for the 60 to 90 time frame is developing a variety of interests during the 25 to 65 years. I have been deeply blessed with opportunities to stretch the brain and exercise the body.

After 27 years of military service, I retired in 1979 at the ripe old age (in military years) of 47. While in the service, I had the opportunity to pursue an advanced degree in psychology/counseling that I eventually turned into a professional career as a family therapist. I could not count the times people asked if I were a psychologist/counselor in the military. When I explained I was an infantry officer it often led to "How did you get into this field?"

After almost 20 years in counseling, I retired again, only to find myself sucked into the quicksand of more than four years producing a weekly column for this newspaper. It is not uncommon for people to inquire about my journalism background. My formal education includes an undergrad degree in agronomy and a masters in school psychology. Writing was embedded in my brain by a high school English teacher named Vera Faulkner (no relation to William) and my interest in people stems from a propensity to be a bit nosy. I would be less than candid if I did not admit that I also enjoy the notoriety.

As a former paratrooper, physical conditioning has always been high among my priorities. After my knees began to decay, I gave up jogging and at 70, took up bicycling. Six months later I did a 100 mile ride around Lake Tahoe. Tennis, hiking and weight lifting round out my physical activities.

This town, I am happy to report, is full of retirees who, like Safire, have just changed jobs. I could name a whole list, but it would be unfair to those I would have to leave off. This may be the most civic-minded, volunteering town in Central Texas—or Texas for that matter. If you want to see a bunch of folks for whom retirement has simply meant a change of jobs, visit the library, the hospital, the senior center, the Chamber of Commerce, the Tourist Information Center, the Food Bank, or any of the churches in town.

I am told the nursing homes are full of people who can't lift themselves out of bed. I'm not judging the wisdom of those folks, but I suspect many could have postponed their admission had they planned for their mental and physical future as well as they planned for their financial future.

I tell people I am going to live to 100. Maybe I will. Maybe I won't. But just in case, I enrolled in a yoga class last week.

An Ode to Growing Old

The years have sped by
And crushed our vow to never grow old
We can wonder and ask why
Remembering days we were brave and bold

We had our days in the limelight
And we ran the good race
We engaged in life's daily fight
And lived to the fullest at a rapid pace

And now, we are on the sideline
Nursing our ailments, aches and pains
Raging against the inevitable events of time
Nostalgically remembering our losses and gains

As we reflect and remember
It often seems we have just begun
But here in Life's cold December
We concede: Growing Old is no fun

Daylight Saving Time

I hate Daylight Saving Time! (Yes, that is the correct spelling—it does not have an "s" on saving.) It is a lie! We don't save any daylight. We just move it from morning to evening. There is only so much daylight in the day. Changing a clock does not in any way affect the rotation of the earth and it's relation to the sun. We are only deluding ourselves when we assume we are making the days longer by moving the hands of the clock forward by one hour.

I get up relatively early Monday, Wednesday and Friday when I'm scheduled to go to the gym. It is around 6:00 A.M. I take great delight in the fact that the sun is beginning to push the darkness over the western horizon by that time in late March. I can ride my bicycle to the gym without fear of being run down by a 4,000 pound SUV with defective headlights. Further, it seems more civilized to be up and about with the sun, rather than groping my way through the streets and guessing at the location of the potholes and street repair barriers.

About the time I get accustomed to having some daylight in the mornings, that dreaded day—the first Sunday in April—shows up and we go through the clock-changing ritual. Or not. In the latter case, we show up an hour late for Sunday School.

As a kid growing up on a farm, we always were up by 6:00, got the milking and other chores done by 7:00 and I really appreciated being able to see where to step so as not to bring the odor of the cow lot to the house and consequently to the school room. If we had used DST, I would have been forced to do those critical chores in the dark and I quite likely would have been redolent with the aroma of the cow pen. That would not have enhanced my popularity. I had enough trouble getting a date.

I can remember that the sun was fully exposed in the east as Ms. Livley's big yellow school bus nosed its way over the cliché road that was our connection to the schoolhouse. Many of my classmates had been on that bus for a half-hour by the time it stopped at our lane. But it was daylight when they boarded it.

Today, school kids—six or seven years old—are at the bus stop before dawn. What must they be thinking as the headlights pierce the darkness in search of that precious cargo? It seems so unfair to the children.

Who benefits from daylight saving time? I have heard rumors that it saves energy, but no one has ever made a case that made sense to me for that argument. What's the difference in turning on the lights an hour earlier in the morning or an hour earlier in the evening? I looked it up on Google and there is an assertion that we save energy, during daylight saving time, but no statistics are cited and no real proof is offered.

That same article pointed out that chicken farmers and dairy farmers have a major issue with the change. You see, chickens and cows do not respond to electronics. They respond to daylight and dark.

The only people I know who benefit from this abomination are golfers. After spending eight hours staring at a computer screen, I suppose it is a great relief to chase a little white pellet around 200 acres of what could be good grazing land. But, even these folks do not really need DST. There are twilight leagues that use glow in the dark golf balls, so who cares if it gets dark a little early.

To add misery to mayhem, in 2007, DST will be even longer. It will begin on the second Sunday in March and end on the first Sunday in November. G.W. Bush signed that bill and it was Nixon who revived DST in 1974. If you had known that in 2004, would you have voted Republican?

There are all sorts of arguments for DST. Among them are crime reduction, fewer accidents, and I suppose, less acne. But, I'm not convinced.

I am inclined to agree with Robertson Davies who wrote in 1947: *"I don't really care how time is reckoned so long as there is some agreement about it, but I object to being told that I am saving daylight when my reason tells me that I am doing nothing of the kind. I even object to the implication that I am wasting something valuable if I stay in bed after the sun has risen. As an admirer of moonlight I resent the bossy insistence of those who want to reduce my time for enjoying it. At the back of the daylight saving scheme, I detect the bony fingered hand of Puritanism, eager to push people into bed earlier and get them up earlier, to make them healthy, wealthy and wise in spite of themselves."* (The Diary of Samuel Marchbanks, 1947, XIX Sunday.)

Father of the Bride

Have you ever felt as out of place as Dan Quayle at a MENSA convention? Have you ever felt as unwelcome as a Palestinian pig farmer in Tel Aviv? Have you ever felt as irrelevant as a turn signal on an Indy 500 Race car? Then you have been the Father of the Bride.

It has been said that even the bride is a marginal player in the wedding; that it is really Mom who, through her daughter, is attempting to prove that the Cinderella story is true and that romance is real. I'm not here to argue that point. I am here to let you know that the father of the bride has one role and one role only. He exists to provide the bottomless pit from which the money flows to finance this gala.

There are a number of critical points in the wedding planning process. First, I suppose, is site selection. I expect selecting the site for the first atomic test required less time and had fewer criteria than the wedding site. The bride, or more likely the mom, wants an idyllic spot. How about a mountain backdrop with a waterfall, set amid fir trees 100 feet tall. There is such a place. It just happens to be located two states away. Transporting the wedding party will keep United Airlines solvent for the next six months.

Keep in mind that the ceremony will last less than an hour.

But the ceremony is not to be treated lightly. Who is in it and who is excluded? For starters, the father of the bride is almost excluded. He escorts the bride down the aisle. She, in the flower of her youth, is dressed in a $5 thousand gown, and has spent the last 24 hours being coiffed, groomed, and preened. He, needing a haircut, is dressed in an ill-fitting, rented tuxedo. He might as well be a cardboard cut-out on wheels. His participation is purely perfunctory.

Then there are the attendants. Bridesmaids, House Party, Flower Girl, Ring Bearer, Maid of Honor, Matron of Honor, ad inifinitum. All these people must receive gifts. Mom and bride have agonized for days over the proper gift for each of these approximately 20 participants. Should it be a small keepsake diamond, set in platinum, a solid gold locket with pictures of the bride and groom or an exclusive James Avery pin, fashioned just for this occasion. What do you mean, $2 hundred each is expensive? This is her day!!

We haven't yet paid the violinist, the pianist, the soloist, the florist, the limo company or, incidentally, the minister. If the father of the bride wants to feel like a one-legged man at a field goal kicking contest, he should try making a suggestion about the flowers, the music or the ritual. Just pay the man and don't forget to tip him well.

The reception follows. Now, we are talking second mortgage. The day after the engagement announcement appears in the local paper, the bank calls the father of the bride and offers a special interest rate.

Everyone in the bride's high school yearbook is invited. Of course, every relative is invited, even those in Tibet; the mailman; the bride's second grade teacher; and the kid who made her cry when she got braces.

The father has absolutely nothing to say about whether the cake will be 10 or 12 tiers. It is also hard to understand why the strawberries must be dyed blue, but he doesn't ask. The Rap Rockin' Hill Billy Blues Bunch doesn't sound like the kind of band one would have at a wedding reception, but if that's what she wants.... All this, with the filet mignon and lobster just about absorbs the home equity.

The chic honeymoon in the unexplored prehistoric Incan regions of Peru, is made possible by the propitious sale of railroad stock left the bride's father by his grandmother 40 years ago. The tearful daughter reports with her first phone call that she was bitten by a tropical spider of unknown identity and her eyes are swollen shut. But not to worry, the doctor will be on the next plane to their location–a week from today.

Meanwhile, the Peruvian Department of Agriculture will not let them leave until the spider had been identified, and all like it eradicated. Please wire money for another fortnight.

Am I Obsolete?

Recently, I heard a radio interview in which demographics were discussed. The interviewee reported with great delight that over fifty per cent of the people who attend stock car races are between the ages of 21 and 54. "A great demographic," he trumpeted enthusiastically. This tends to bear out what I have been reading lately about TV programmers, networks, radio stations, writers and advertisers and where they aim the majority of their programming. The purpose behind targeting this group is, as Willie Sutton once remarked, when asked why he robbed banks, "That's where the money is."

This realization somehow made me mad. I felt as if I were being told I am no longer of interest to the movers and shakers. I am well past the cut-off age which marks the valued membership group of this country. There is an implication that entertainers, the media, and advertisers no longer care about me. Washed up, over the hill, used goods, yesterday's newspaper, passed by, all those metaphors raced through my mind. The more I thought about it, the angrier I became.

Am I obsolete? Do I and all my contemporaries who have survived fifty-four or more winters hold no interest for the people who sell things? Is there a Great Computer somewhere that knows our birthdates and when we reach the magic number, deletes us from the files of the meaningful. Is there a Great Junk Yard of No Longer Relevant People. Are we sent there like an old car to rust away, quietly and unobtrusively? Are Scottsdale, St. Petersburg, and Miami Beach the Great Junk Yards of America?

Did anyone ever tell Winston Churchill he was obsolete? Did Konrad Adenauer, Golda Mieir, and Joseph Stalin know they were obsolete? How about Tolstoy, Shaw and DeGaulle? What do the movers and shakers think happens to the over 54 set? Do they think we suddenly become blind, deaf, and without resources?

The country is so obsessed with the young the movers and shakers would like to deny the existence of the growning numbers of a mature generation. "Mature" is an euphemism for "old". Personally, I am old. There will soon be more of us than there are of them. But what makes us invisible is that we don't dictate what's HOT and what's not. The focus is on everything from crime to entertainment. Sports, politics, religion, art and literature all have their Wunderkinder leading the way to bigger, better, greater, more stupendous things. Martina Hingis is the world's number one women's tennis player before she is 18; Ralph Reed, a thirty-something is the most influential religious conservative in the country; Alexandra Nechita, a sub-teen, is touted as the next Picasso; and a 13 year-old inner city child is hailed as the next Hemingway. So here I sit somewhere midway between my first social security check and my first box of Depends and I feel as though some would like to delete me from the realm of the real.

Before my knees turned traitor on me, I routinely beat kids half my age at tennis–took three sets sometimes; I get up at 6:00 AM almost every day and work out with a gym full of twenty-somethings who stare at me with envy and amazement. I dream of the day when I get my little red sports car. I think more clearly, I have more patience, I am saner, I experience deeper enjoyment and I have more money than I have ever had and when the movers and shakers imply I'm obsolete, it makes me mad as hell. I want all us AARPs over 54 to crank up those $200,000.00 RV's and go out there and spend our 21 to 54 year old kids' inheritance on bird watching, cryonics, burial sites on the moon and any other unreasonable and ridiculous idea you can bring to mind. Let's drive them mad!

Reunions

If you are younger than 60 years old, you need not read any further.

The weekend of October 26 and 27, I attended an informal reunion in Brenham for my college class (Texas A&M, 1952). We call these informal reunions mini-reunions and they have been an annual event since I can remember. They supplement the regular five-year official get-togethers. Inasmuch as we are all past 75 years of age, you can imagine it is hardly the energetic and raucous affair of years ago. Nevertheless, we still have an open bar, we dress in as much maroon and white as we can wear, and we express our loyalty as only Aggies can.

Because of my military career, I was often too far away to attend for the first 25 years or so, but since my retirement, I have been a fairly regular attendee.

On the subject of reunions, I have the opportunity to attend several each year. Most of them involve military units with which I served. The locations range from Washington, D.C. to Fort Benning, Georgia to Fort Riley, Kansas, Chicago and San Francisco. I have attended some from time to time. Others, I have never attended. Where reunions are concerned, military people tend to be like the swallows of Capistrano. They are likely to return until death or infirmities restrict their abilities. I do not count myself among the regulars.

The Aggie mini-reunions last a couple of days and are usually scheduled around a football game. There was a time when one would not think of going to the reunion without going to the game. A bus was chartered and most of us piled on the bus with an ample supply of adult beverages to get in the "spirit" before the game and to enhance our celebration on the way home in case the Aggies won. In case we lost, we could induce an alcoholic amnesia and think about next year. For the past few years, wide-screen televisions have been available at the hotel in Brenham for those who can no longer get to their stadium seats with a walker or whose breathing is seriously affected by the climb to the second tier of Kyle Field. The wide-screen televisions have made chartering a bus unnecessary.

Our mini-reunions have become rather predictable. There are between 50 and 60 (some 800 of 1100 grads are still alive, I understand) of us who regularly attend the Brenham gatherings. I call them The Usual Suspects. This year two came from as far away as Colorado. We have had attendees from California and perhaps farther away. We also have classmates who live in Brenham and do not attend the reunions. I can't explain the motivation for maintaining these ancient contacts and friendships. Perhaps it is our way of denying our own mortality for the stories we exchange about classmates that have passed and those that are absent due to some infirmity are overshadowed by the exchange of campus memories of more than 50 years ago; memories of when we were young and vital and faced an uncertain future.

There is always the possibility of a surprise. This year I saw a classmate I had not seen since we crossed the stage with our diplomas and commissions at graduation.

I took my four yearbooks (1949–1952) to Brenham. It would take a PhD paleontologist to identify some of us today from our pictures in those books. Teeth and hair are missing. Hearing aids and eye glasses are prevalent. Some of the svelte, handsome guys of the late 40's, early 50's carry a lot of extra pounds around the middle. Wrinkles have distended those formerly handsome facial features. But the attitude, personality and general demeanor remain. We haven't changed that much.

Our conversations have changed somewhat. In the early years, we talked about ourselves; later we talked about our kids or grandkids. Now, we talk about our cardiologist, our urologist, and our orthopedic surgeon.

Many of our classmates have become super successful financially. But, a stranger would never be able to identify them in the crowd. There's something about being among that group that transports all of us back to the days when Texas A&M enrollment was just short of 6,000, there were no women students on campus, and all able-bodied students, except the veterans of WWII, were in the Corps of Cadets. The only class distinction I ever saw at A&M was that defined by tradition of seniority. That is, the seniors, juniors and sophomores had distinctive privileges based on class. The freshmen had no privileges.

Because our football team was less than overwhelmingly successful when we were students, it was common for us to often repeat the phrase, "Wait 'til next year." Our mini-reunions *are* overwhelmingly successful, and I can hardly "Wait 'til next year."

Cell Phones

I know, I know! Cell phones are a nuisance and the people who use them are unthinking boors. The users talk too loud; the phones go off in church or the theater; conversations can never be completed without a cell phone interruption; many automobile accidents are the results of people using cell phones while driving. So, the ubiquitous cell phone plague is the price we pay for modern-day technology

My 15 year-old grandson has a cell phone. He can text-message, send an e-mail, take a picture, store phone numbers, and, for all I know, determine his longitude and latitude at any given moment. I have finally mastered answering a call and making a call. He thinks I'm a Neanderthal

As with almost everything, however, there is another side to this phenomenon. It seldom is talked about, but, even for me—a technological illiterate—there is an upside to this weirdness.

In the beginning there was the car phone. I must admit, my wife and I had lived together 20 + years without a portable phone of any sort. About 15 years ago, our daughter gave birth to the aforementioned grandson. At the time, Jamie, the daughter, was employed as a flight attendant. Since baby-sitters were: 1) difficult to find; 2) more difficult to schedule; and 3) proved grossly unreliable, guess who volunteered to drive almost 200 miles one-way to baby-sit. Yep, Grandmother drew the short straw.

One-hundred seventy-five miles on I-10 and 25 miles through the heart of Houston loomed as a rather daunting undertaking for a woman driving alone, so, as a safety measure, I reluctantly agreed that a portable phone would be a practical acquisition. In 1993, car phones were about the size of a small Igloo ice chest. They hooked to the cigarette lighter outlet of the car.

It doesn't take long for a convenience to become a necessity, i.e., television, vacuum cleaners, microwave ovens, etc. My wife grew accustomed to having a phone in the car, so, even after there was no need for her to drive to Houston, she insisted that a portable phone was essential.

As technology improved and phones were no longer tethered to the cigarette lighter plug, she began to refer to our car phone as a paleontological; relic; a museum piece; and an embarrassing carbuncle on the nose of progress.

OK, so, we—she—signed up for a mobile phone. I don't think they were called cell phones at the time. That worked well.

And, that is the point of this article. In spite of all the bad-mouthing engendered by cell phones, there is a place for them and they have, in general, added to our safety and security, not to mention the convenience they offer.

A few years ago, when I began riding more than five miles on my bicycle, my wife insisted I take her phone with me in the event, of an accident, or some other untoward incident. I rode with her phone for a couple of years and I remember calling her once. I had a flat and the spare tube, would not inflate properly. She came for me.

About a year ago, I discovered Go Phones, a cheap alternative to a permanent plan. It serves my need for a safety net when riding long distances or when I'm traveling alone.

While I can't recall an instance where the phone has been employed to rescue one of us from a serious incident, there have been hundreds of times when it proved quite reassuring and provided a much appreciated peace of mind.

Minor conveniences derived from the cell phone abound: Calling from the grocery store to verify the need for something. Or more likely, the list says "cereal" and you discover that there are 400 varieties of "cereal' in the cereal aisle; letting someone know you are stuck in traffic and you will be late; searching for an address and having someone on the phone who can direct you to the spot; the sound of a friendly voice is extremely reassuring when one's keys are locked in the car...with the motor running.

In addition, we can call San Marcos from Colorado and it's a local call.

So, when you become annoyed at someone's obnoxious phone behavior, keep in mind that maybe—just maybe—someone else is feeling reassured.

Jury Duty

The Official Jury Summons arrived around May 30, greeting me and informing that I was:...HEREBY SUMMONED TO BE AND APPEAR IN PERSON BEFORE: THE COUNTY COURT on Monday, June 16, 2014 at 8:45 AM.

I was also informed that the court is located at the Government Center (commonly called the Taj Mahal) on Stagecoach Trail.

I take these things seriously. As I was to later find out, not everyone does. I noted the date on my calendar; activated my phone reminder and told all who would listen, so that I would not forget this civic responsibility.

I immediately answered the very brief questionnaire that accompanied the summons, filed the double sheet summons in a fool-proof location and smugly took a certain pride in the opportunity to perform a civic duty, that, in my opinion, overrides voting as an obligatory responsibility.

The summons contained a fairly exhaustive list of reasons one can be excused from jury duty. Number one among the reasons was "the individual is over 70 years of age." Then there were other reasons, such as, responsibility for a child under 12 y/o; medical considerations; enrolled in an institution of higher learning, etc.

Obviously, I met the first criterion; however, I was eager to serve. My age has not eroded my desire to perform my civic duty, especially as it applies to local matters.

On Monday morning, June 16, 2014, I arrived at the Government Center and located County Courtroom 1, the designated place of assembly for prospective jurors. Since this was a government operation, I was not expecting precise timing and immaculate efficiency, however, I was hoping for a relatively small time gap between 8:45 AM and the appearance of an official to organize, inform and seat the assembled group of concerned citizens.

At around 9:00 AM, a young woman with a clipboard and a young male assistant managed to get us in an orderly line and one by one, collected our questionnaires. Not bad. Fifteen minutes cushion is tolerable and understandable because I'm sure the 8:45 time was intentional to give those who are not afflicted with the promptness virus a flexible arrival time.

The card collection and seating went remarkably well. I, with crutches in hand, managed to stay comfortable on a hallway bench until near the very end of the line.

Once inside Courtroom 1, the well-oiled wheels of justice ground slowly to a halt. After approximately 30 minutes with no action, other than two lawyers, each diligently reviewing an impressive stack of paper that I presumed to be pertinent to the pending case, the presiding judge appeared.

Sans robe, the judge was very casually dressed. In a friendly, apologetic tone, he announced that we were waiting for his court reporter who had detoured to rescue her husband whose car had stalled on his way to work. And that we would be trying a civil case. A room full of mostly employment age citizens, forgoing their own employment, to answer the jury summons, waited patiently for a court functionary to tend to a personal matter.

Before he disappeared back into his sanctuary, the judge gave us permission to stand, stretch, go out to the hallway and just relax. While that probably got him some personality points, it did nothing to move the jury selection along.

It says a lot about the respect we have for the court system that there were no loud boos of disapproval; no preemptory walking out of court; and no snide remarks audible throughout the room.

It wasn't long before the court reporter showed up and busied herself with her equipment before disappearing through the same door. We assumed the lawyers would begin the voir dire (jury selection) process momentarily. Bad assumption.

Silence, broken only by the hum of muffled conversations, once again filled the room. The lawyers continued with their study of their paperwork, the bailiff moved back and forth at the behest of the clerks and lawyers. At this point, we began to look at each other a little more furtively and facial expressions began to change from quizzical to questioning.

After another 30 minutes the bailiff took both lawyers through the door from which the judge had earlier emerged. They returned to the courtroom forthwith and without explanation went immediately to the hallway.

The lawyers returned and went back through the door to the Rabbit Hole where people disappeared and returned without reason or explanation.

We have now been in the courtroom/courthouse some one and a half hours and nothing resembling a judicial process has occurred.

Shortly, the judge, again, sans robe, made an appearance. This time, he made a short speech about the importance of jury duty; the responsibility attached thereto; and complimented those of us who showed up. During this appearance, he announced that 250 summons had been mailed; 53 people were present in the room, giving us a 20 percent response from those summoned.

The stunning part of the announcement was when he said, "This (the 20 percent showing) is about average for this court."

It was then that he announced that neither the plaintiff, nor the defendant had appeared nor would they appear, therefore he dismissed all of us.

I am still puzzled, disappointed and maybe, even, shocked by these events.

So many unanswered questions: How can it be that only one out of five people summoned for jury duty shows up? There is a penalty, but that begs the question: Is it enforced? Were the plaintiff and the defendant held in contempt of court, and if so, what will be the penalty? Is this a common occurrence?

The dismissal was welcome, in view of all that went before, but one wonders about the economics of such events. At $6.00 a day, the county was not out much in salary for the prospective jurors, but there is a judge, a court reporter, bailiff, clerk(s) and miscellaneous. For what?

Am I upset that I went to court when I could have been automatically excused? No. Emphatically, no.

Jury duty is a duty! Fifty-three people answered the call to serve. Our system is not perfect and in this case, it failed—more or less. But it is the best system in the world. Justice is a concern to the people of Hays County, even if only one in five responds to its call. That is enough to insure that it will endure and that our guilt or innocence will be determined by a *jury of our peers.* Long may it wave!

Great Texas Trails Monument

Last Friday's edition of the Daily Record carried a front page story, with an illustration yet, of the proposed Great Texas Trails Monument. The lead paragraph of the story reads: "The feasibility of The Great Texas Trails Monument will be discussed Monday night at City Council." So, by the time you read this, the discussion will have occurred.

Seems to me the council could have better spent that time discussing the merits of annexing Martindale and de-annexing Westover. The road situation might improve in both locations. I would really like to see all that road machinery, located at Bishop and Brown Streets, moved to the east side of town.

The question in my mind was: What's to discuss about this proposed monument to UGLY? I notice that a task force of 10 San Marcos citizens traveled to Kearney, Nebraska to research the Great Platte River Road Archway Monument. As I recall most of the task force members' comments ranged from serious doubt to outright opposition to the Texas Trails project.

Well, it seems the City Council listened to the task force and cancelled any further discussion of the Great Texas Trails Monument. Let's give them an A+ for that decision. Now if we can just get the same kind of cooperation and action concerning traffic control in the city.

The developers of that monument are Jeff and Greg Smith, brothers, I presume. The last time I heard of the Smith Brothers, they were a bearded pair, think ZZ TOP, selling cherry flavored cough drops. Probably no relation, but imagine the crowd at City Hall if the Smiths had showed up with ZZ TOP beards and a guitar.

In earlier stories about this monstrosity, the Smiths were quoted that no public funds would be required to build it. Well...maybe a couple mil as seed money to get it underway. My experience tells me the city does not have funds to synchronize traffic lights, so are we going to find $2 million in change under the sofa cushions?

My real concern is not that we would build the thing and it would be a failed eyesore. I firmly believe in the H.L. Mencken adage: "No one ever went broke underestimating the taste of the American public." I was really scared the thing might be a successful eyesore. The IH-35 Austin/San Antonio corridor is already the world's longest parking lot.

Would we really want to attract the kind of people who would visit a monument like that? I think we have enough diversity in San Marcos. If a recent emigre from Minnesota wanted to learn about the historic Texas cattle drives, he could always rent the John Wayne movie, Red River. Or get the DVD set of Lonesome Dove.

If the Smith boys still want to put up something to attract a lot of people, to a place that needs them, I suggest they go out to Snyder and erect a 400 foot oil derrick across I-20. They need the tourists, and to the folks out there, anything that suggests oil and money in the same sentence is absolutely beautiful.

If we ever decide to do something certifiably stupid, let's import the World's Biggest Ball of Twine. Know where that is? Didn't think so.

It's in Cawker City, Kansas and they hold a Twine-a-Thon every year to add to it. They have a picnic, a parade and a twine winding. (Would I make this up?) Talk about excitement. Can't you just see 1,000 Harley's barreling down IH-35 with their jack-booted riders, snarling and salivating to be the first to get their twine on that big ball.

Aren't you glad the City Council de-horned that Great Texas Trails Monument?

Concrete Cowboy

He doesn't ride and he doesn't rope
The cowboy part is just a joke
He owns a ranch or maybe three
But herding cows ain't his cup o' tea

He can fly a plane and drive a truck
But he'd be off a horse in just one buck
He loves the land and what it means
So, he plays the part in boots and jeans

Once described as an easy-going guy
His daughter said, "That's a lie!
Behind that smile there's will of steel
He's tough as a bull and slick as an eel"

He is not who he was born to be
He took another name as a result of tragedy
But never has he shied from life's heavy demands
His fate is always determined by his own hands

An ambitious young man, education was dear
His desire was to be an Aggie engineer
Two years later, he was invited to leave
Parsing a sentence was more than he could achieve

The navy beckoned and he answered the call
He learned construction and equipment and savored it all

Four years later, he began a career
That would occupy him for many a year

He took his young bride to Dilley
And though some may think it quite silly
He paid a little boy a nickel an hour that year
To keep her company and waylay her fear

A second-hand concrete plant and two old trucks
Gave him a start that would clear a few bucks
He worked all day and part of the night
To stay out of debt and make things right

He has poured concrete from Laredo to Austin
Some say his total would reach from L.A. to Boston
Those hundreds of black and yellow trucks on the road
Are Ready-Mix vehicles delivering another load

The Concrete Cowboy is now seventy-five
So, kick back, take a break, while you're alive
"What would I do?" says he
"Golf, dominoes and fishing are not for me"

For the Cowboy, living is working and working is living
He and Gloria are known for their generous giving
So don't bother asking when he's going to quit
He doesn't know, 'cause Gloria has to approve of it

We hope you are enjoying your day
We've run out of anything else to say
So, Happy Birthday and Many More
You are one of a kind—there are no others in store

Bibb Underwood
for Bruce
July 2005

Garage Sales

Garage sales seem to be a rather widespread phenomenon these days. I don't know when they came into vogue. I know as a kid we never had them. We had a use for everything. We wore clothes until they wore out. We played with toys until they broke. If we had an extra piece of furniture, which I don't remember we ever had, we loaned it or gave it to a neighbor. If something broke, we fixed it or threw it away. We would never think of selling it to a neighbor. So, what do garage sales say about us and why do we patronize them?

First, we have a lot more stuff than we need. Look in almost any woman's closet today and she could fill a sizable portion of the front lawn with shoes alone. Until I was 40 years old, I had 'Sunday' shoes and 'everyday shoes.' Now, I have three pairs of tennis shoes. I'm not telling how many other pairs of shoes I have, but it is way too many. Clothes alone at garage sales seem to constitute a good part of the merchandise, but I have yet to know of anyone who ever purchased a piece of clothing at a garage sale. Do they? How many of you, dear readers, (I hope there's more than one) have said in the last three months, "I need to clean out the attic/basement/garage and have a garage sale." I thought so. You can put your hands down now.

Second, many of us are motivated by the Wille Sutton (a 50's era bank robber) syndrome. We have a little–OK, a lot–of LARCENY in our heart. That's what motivates us. We are determined to get something for nothing–or next to nothing.

If we sponsor it, the garage sale gives us an opportunity to see how many people we can get to give us good money for a piece of useless, to us, material that has been taking up space and collecting dust at our house for three years. Conversely, we go to garage sales looking for that treasure–a lamp, a picture, a chair, a sofa, that brand new crescent wrench, all the Harry Potter books, a Faulkner paperback that is out of print–for a steal. And I use the word 'steal' advisedly. That is what we are trying to do. We all have this urge to steal legally. We want to get something for nothing.

Third, we like to inspect other people's trash. I guess, along with Willie Sutton, there is a little J. Edgar Hoover in us. Remember when Hoover had highly trained FBI investigators inspecting the trash of Martin Luther King, Frank Sinatra and others. Go to a garage sale and you will often hear in hushed tones, "I can't believe she ever had that in her house. I wouldn't give that to my mother-in-law." And speaking of trash, that is often where a lot of our garage sale purchases end up. We get it home, plug it in and find out why it was in the garage sale in the first place. It doesn't work. It can be repaired, but that would cost more than a new one.

Fourth, some people go to garage sales to get material for their garage sale. This I believe. We see the same people at all garage sales and I know they could not possibly use some of the stuff they buy. What are they doing with it? Putting it in their garage sale. Not only do we see the same people at garage sales, we see the same stuff: the bicycle with flat tires and no chain, an end table with a broken leg, the kitchen gadget which no one could ever guess its primary use. It is still in the original box (batteries not included). There is also a set of wrenches which will only fit a 1957 Austin-Healy. And there is a portable mixer with no blades. Clothes, don't forget the clothes. If you were trying to costume the cast of "Bye, Bye Birdie" or "Grapes of Wrath," you might find just what you need. But there are clothes, lots of clothes. Before I become too derisive of garage sale clothes, I suppose, in the interest of veritas, I should admit I'm wearing a really nice leather belt I found for fifty cents in a recent garage sale.

Fifth, and I believe this is really the only viable reason to have or participate in a garage sale. Money changes hands without the government getting a cut. Almost all transactions are handled in cash. There is no license, no inventory, no receipts, no profit and loss, no payroll withholding, and no workmen's comp to provide an auditor with a handhold of suspicion, concerning your activity. It is here on Saturday, gone on Monday. So, if for no other reason, Vive la garage sales. Long may they wave.

Accident

The stockinged foot upon the stair
Searched for a step that was not there
Nylon to nylon, there was no grip
Legs and arms akimbo, it was a painful trip

At the foot of the stairs she lay immobile
Her body in pain, her position ignoble
Her grey-green eyes blurred and filled with tears
Her mind was gripped with awful fears

A struggle to the phone to relay her plight
The sobs in her voice betrayed her fright
"I can stand, I can walk but I can not bend
I think I've broken my own rear end."

Crawling and kneeling, scrambling to the car
To the doctor, she's lucky it's not very far
Face down, bottom up, she looks at the floor
She quips, "traveling this way is really a bore."

The doctor confirms, "You've broken your coccyx"–
A thing needed long ago for climbing up trees and over rockses
A small triangular bone, shaped like a cuckoo's beak
It's utterly useless unless you're a tree-climbing freak

There's no way to treat the pesky little thing
For it's physically impossible to put your ass in a sling

The only way possible to mend this little bone
Is to make sure your position is always the prone

Ten days like that and she's ready for a crate
She snarls at her child, she growls at her mate
Sick people on game shows and soap operas so sad
Mundane talk shows and news that's inevitably bad

Her chin gets raw and her elbows get a scab
Getting in or out of bed, she crawls like a crab
Should anyone <u>ever</u> offer the toast, Bottoms Up
He should immediately choke on his infernal cup

Compliments

This year, I resolved to compliment someone every chance I get, even when they are only doing their job. They might be doing it with a migraine.

Compliments are probably the least expensive and most effective means of creating loyalty and good will and motivating people. Here, I enter my disclaimer. I realize one must be a bit wary these days about comments which can be interpreted as sexist or racist, but don't you think most people know sincerity when they see or hear it?

Compliments are a way of showing approval and who among us doesn't want approval? Self-esteem is built on the knowledge that others approve of our looks, activity, personality, dress, and behavior. It derives from the respect we get from our peers, our mates, our employees, and our employers. That is not to say that we need to spend all our energy trying to please others. That robs us of our individuality and our creativity. We need to have boundaries to define who we are. Nevertheless, the approval of others is crucial to our mental health. Depression often results from the feeling that we are unappreciated and that what we are doing is unimportant.

Compliments are a powerful tool. Have you ever noticed how a person's countenance can change with just a few words? "That's a pretty blouse" can wipe a scowl off a person's face almost as quickly as "I like your new hair style." Compliments can change a relationship. If you are having difficulty with someone at work, in your social circle, club, or church, I guarantee you can change that person's attitude toward you with a few well chosen remarks. Probably the most powerful compliment one can get is to hear something positive about his/her children. Frequently, a simple question inquiring about a child's welfare will sound like a compliment to a parent.

I get a great deal of pleasure passing along compliments to people who do not hear enough of them. A store clerk who helps me locate a three-quarter inch thingamajig to repair the broken whatchamacallit has done a real service for me, especially when he reminds me that this particular part has a left-handed thread and should always be installed top-side up. I am frequently awed by the skill of some craftsmen. A tree-trimmer who, while hanging upside down, takes meticulous care to shape my 100 year old oak is a pure artist and I want to tell him so. My auto mechanic, who is paid a rather substantial hourly wage, is, in my view, still eager to know I appreciate his checking the freon as well as the brake fluid.

The military makes a habit of passing out compliments. They call them medals. They are official recognition of a person's deeds. Some are for bravery, others are for showing up every day. Medals are tangible compliments employed by the military to enhance morale, insure fidelity, and let the wearer understand that his/her actions have been officially noted. Every medal in the military, except one, can be awarded for simply doing well what is expected of you. The Congressional Medal of Honor is the only military medal which requires the recipient to perform 'above and beyond' the call of duty.

We should look for opportunities to pass along a compliment. At the construction site, the flagman who holds that little two-sided STOP/SLOW sign may not be seriously challenged by his job description. He may not be the most creative guy in the crew and you may think he is overpaid for what he does. But when he stops you in the middle of the road, or requires you to slow to a virtual crawl, make that an opportunity to tell him how important his job is and how well he is doing it. He may be doing it with a migraine.

Phone Books

We take telephone books for granted. They are a ubiquitous fixture in offices and households. Every household and every office has a phone book. It is, of course, a natural consequence of Alexander Graham Bell's invention. Today, I suppose it would be called an unintended consequence. I'm sure no one set out to create the encyclopedic entity that it has become. It is literally a census of a given area.

There was a time, long, long ago when we had no need for a phone book. We did not need a phone book for two reasons. First, there was no phone in the office or household. Second, if there were a phone, one picked up the receiver, gave a short ring and "central" came on the line. One simply told "central," who was probably Ida Bell Smith, to ring Momma 'n 'em. Ida Bell not only knew who was calling, she knew if Momma 'n 'em were home or if they were playing dominoes at the Rogers' house. And she could ring the Rogers' house if you asked her. That is, if the line to the Rogers' house were working.

Phone books contain information we all take for granted. A cursory reading of the phone book gives one a reasonable idea of the ethnic make-up of a given area. Names reveal countries of origin, ancestral connections and, often, secondary languages. This information, in turn, reveals cultural aspects of the area. It gives major clues as to the types of businesses, especially restaurants, that might be found in abundance in the area. One might surmise the popularity of certain religions in the region from a reading of the surnames.

As a writer, I use the phone book as a spelling dictionary. I write a name, the spelling of which is apparent. Well...maybe not so apparent. I often ask people to spell names as I conduct an interview, but occasionally, I forget. So, I start writing John Doe. Wait a minute is that John or Jon; Doe or Dowe or Dough or Deaux. The phone book usually has the answer.

If you are passing through an area and want to look up an old friend, the phone book will direct you. First, it will reveal his presence, unless he is one of those who is so self-important he has an unlisted number. You didn't want to call him anyway. With his address, you can make an educated guess about his life-style. If he lives on Sweet Gum Glen or on Balmoral Circle, he is in the burbs. Every other house is a Tudor and there is an abundance of Expeditions, 4 Runners and Suburbans parked in front of the Turdor. On the other hand, if your friend's address is 313 South 4th., you can pretty well imagine he is not too far from the fire station, and he is in walking distance of the donut shop. In San Marcos, it would be helpful to know where *historical* Belvin Street ends and Belvin street begins.

If there is a number for Amber and Justin, same surname, same address, he/she has two teen-age kids.

In the Blue Pages, our San Marcos phone book offers an abridged Chamber of Commerce pitch for the city and surrounding areas. And one can get the phone number to any facility imaginable. The blue pages offer a categorization of facilities, i.e., recreation, educational, sports, investments, arts and cultural, financial, legal, political, ad infinitum.

Our phone book contains a cross reference of numbers. So, if you wrote a number on your note pad yesterday and can't remember today who it belongs to, (especially important to 60's and over) you can look up the number, locate the name and save yourself some embarrassment. That is, if you can remember the phone book has the cross reference.

How many times a day does the average person use the phone book? I have no idea, but even with today's data storing electronic gadgets, I surmise that the average business person or domestic executive (formerly housewife) uses the phone book at least three times a day. Is it the most essential publication in the country?

The yellow pages are significant beyond my ability to describe. When your dishwasher is making like Niagra Falls—with suds—where do you turn? To the yellow pages, of course. When you are in the mood for a make-over, there are three pages of beauty salon listings. That doesn't count cosmetologists, aerobic instructors or weight loss programs. And do the publishers have a sense of irony? Marital counselors are listed next to martial arts instructors who are listed just before massage therapists who are followed by mattress companies.

There is more, but I must go. My daughter is calling. She can't find the phone book.

Mothers Day

This column is a week late and my editor said, "What else is new, Bibb?" While it should have appeared last week, I often find myself mentally composing the column I should have written on the day it should have appeared in the paper. To clarify that run-on sentence, it was already Mothers Day when I had the idea for this column.

As I mused about the Mothers Day observance, May 10, I reflected on my own maternal forbearers and concluded that I am a very lucky man. Were I to honor the women in my life who have been mother figures to me, I would have four gracious, generous, untiring women whose influence guided me along the way.

First, there was my mother, Vera Akers Underwood. She was a bright, serious, over-taxed, hard-working woman. She was a sad woman, it seemed. I may have mistaken her seriousness for sadness, but I think not. She had reason to be sad. She was married to a man and with three surviving children, she saw no way out. Another reason for her permanent melancholy was the loss of her oldest child, a daughter, who died in a tragic accident at the age of three.

She taught me to work hard, be frugal and save for a rainy day. And for school clothes and whatever else I might want or need. She taught me to expect disappointments in life and to keep going anyway. She taught me to be honest, to persevere and to hope for the best... and to clean my plate.

She taught me to serve. When an itinerant Mexican, who spent the day bent over in the cotton fields, came to our door well after dark and inquired, "Tiene una carte para Lopez?" (She was the postmaster of Millersiview), she never turned him away.

Next, there was my second, third and fourth grade teacher, Nellie Bryson. Yes, she taught me all three grades. She was probably 40 when she taught me and I thought she was old. She raised two daughters, went back to school and began a career in teaching. She taught me to add, subtract and spell.

Did she ever teach me to spell? Bobbie Jo Rainwater (Underwood and Rainwater—sounds like a course in range management) and I won the Concho County Meet in spelling one year. We won because Nellie Bryson drilled us day after day with a sample list of words. We spelled at recess, we spelled after school and we spelled before school. She also taught me to study hard and to believe I could succeed. She taught me to respect others. She taught me discipline and to not chew gum in class.

The third person who had a motherly influence over me was Vera Faulkner, my high school English teacher. Small, bent from osteoporosis, allergic to everything, she suffered the dust and pollen and smoke from burning cotton burrs, to bring Dickens, Shakespeare, and Hemingway to a bunch of farm kids whose knowledge of the outside world ended at the McCulloch County line. She taught me to think and to put those thoughts on paper. She taught me where to put commas and periods so that others could understand those thoughts.

What she really taught me was that the world did not end at the McCulloch County line. One day, she handed me an application to enter Texas A&M and said, "Fill this out." It was not a request. She was a powerful presence, in spite of her physical appearance. Having no children of her own, she adopted all of us. I don't ever remember her raising her voice in class. She did not need to. When she spoke, we listened.

She taught me the parts of speech and the importance of education. She taught me dedication and self-sacrifice.

The last time I saw her she was in the fatal clutches of Parkinson's disease. It had drawn her limbs into her body and she was no bigger than a basketball, it seemed. Her husband had to translate all her utterances. I drove away from her house and stopped on a country lane and cried until no tears remained. That memory still brings a flood.

The fourth mother I encountered was Aunt Molly Smith, my mother's younger sister. I was 13 when my first mother died from a household accident. I and my two sisters were unsure what would happen to us when the tragedy occurred. But, Aunt Molly stepped up and volunteered to take us. She and Uncle Bill were childless and though it was not by choice, I'm not sure they really wanted children until we came along.

Aunt Molly taught me to be resourceful. Sacks for the cow feed came in printed material and I often wore underwear that matched my shirt. She could sew a dress for my younger sister between the time she came home from school (she taught for awhile) and bedtime.

She taught me that there is never too much to do. She could feed 12 combine hands at dinner, drive a load of maize to the elevator in Brady, milk 2-3 cows, feed the chickens, gather the eggs and feed the hogs and fix supper, and then sew the dress before bedtime.

She taught me that a sense of humor is essential for a healthy attitude. She loved to gamble and she could play poker, pick a horse race or bet a football game. Win or lose, she could laugh at her luck or lack of it.

She also taught me that chocolate chip cookies and cold milk will cure about anything.

While, it is a week after Mothers Day, I think it is never too late to honor these sainted women. I hope that those of you who read this column will reflect on the mothers you have encountered. Perhaps you will pause briefly and recall how they blessed your life. If it evokes a tear or two, my purpose will have been served.

Broken Computer

Until I went to college, we did not have a phone in the house. We watched for the mail to arrive by rural carrier six days a week. If we wanted a new pair of shoes, we often ordered them from the catalogue and waited two weeks for them to arrive. If we had something to tell someone, we stopped by his or her house when coming or going somewhere else. We often asked a passing neighbor to 'tell Mr. Fowler I'll be there tomorrow to cut that 40 acres of maize on the south side of his place.'

My grandfather ran a grocery store with a pencil and paper. He bought cotton for Anderson-Clayton the same way. When I was about eight, my closest friend and I lived about a half-mile apart and we learned a code of yelling to send messages to each other. Life was simple. It moved at a leisurely pace.

However, I am learning how quickly we not only acclimate, but become totally dependent on technology. Yesterday, my computer broke. As a result I am suffering withdrawal and experiencing serious anxiety.

In the short time I have been without it, I have discovered a computer is not just a machine. It is a connection to the world. In seconds I can go to California or Colorado to visit my friends. I have enough information at my literal finger tips to overflow the Library of Congress. I can order a book or a boat and have it delivered in three days. I can write voluminous letters and send them to the recipients in seconds. I can find the address of old army buddies, normally long since forgotten.

When my car is broken, I can't go to the grocery store, or drop in on a neighbor, or take care of an overdue errand. Inconvenient, yes, but hardly demoralizing.

The computer brings a list of capabilities into my home. It has become more than a luxury. It has become a necessity. I do all my bookkeeping, writing, journaling, and game playing on the computer. So, it has become a necessity. In the way the telephone, the dishwasher and the television have become necessities. It is a necessity only because we expect to have these things. However, the expectation has become so ingrained, the items seem to be essential.

With my computer broken, I become disoriented. I no longer have a reason to take leave of whatever activity is engaging my attention and check my email. This I do about six times a day. Nor can I send a quick and passing email thought, before I forget it, to a friend in Colorado. I am reminded of the discomfort I felt when I quit smoking. I had time that I was unaccustomed to. I had to find something to do with my hands.

There is no medical library. I am denied my trip to the Internet with my latest symptoms in search of a diagnosis. I'm forced to content myself with my doctor's prognostication of acute heartburn with gastric complications resulting from ingesting rich, over cooked, over seasoned foods. Imbibing certain adult beverages also contribute to the situation. If I had my computer, I could find at least 12 serious heart disorders to which my symptoms would point.

I can no longer access every airline schedule in the world. I have no way of checking the cost, frequency and space availability on Air India to Bangladesh during the month of August. Not that I want to go to Bangladesh, but it is reassuring to know that if I did want to go, I could leave Houston on Wednesday and be in Khulna on Friday by way of London, Dakar, Cairo and Delhi for a mere $7,000.00. Round trip.

Game playing is an important part of owning a working computer. It helps put my mind in neutral while others think I'm actually working on the bills or writing something worthwhile. Free Cell is my favorite computer game. It is a simple little card game–a sophisticated version of Solitaire. When the mind is overloaded, just click on Free

Cell and zombie out. It even has a feature which helps one know when to pay close attention. Lights will blink when only one play is left. It also informs one when there are no more plays left. That eliminates your having to pore over every card to determine you are beat.

Most important, my computer is where my stuff is. It contains everything you ever want to know about my financial status. I have almost come to think that my money is in the computer. It contains my daily schedule. What am I supposed to do today?

Where am I supposed to be? What does the future hold for me? It also contains my journal. How am I to find out what I have done, what I thought yesterday and how do I recapture those meandering thoughts I wrote while I was not playing Free Cell.

I have almost 1,000 addresses and phone numbers of people. Some I am in frequent touch with. Some I haven't seen in 10 years. There are those whose names I do not recognize at all, and others who possibly no longer exist. My computer contains all my letters, articles, notes and poems. In short, my computer is the repository of the record of my life.

So, when my computer is broken, I feel as though my lifeline has been severed temporarily. I have to learn a new way of getting through the day. I may be forced to take up golf. Heaven forbid. I may even get a deck of Bicycle playing cards and see if I remember solitaire. Or, it is possible, I'll see if I can engage my wife in conversation.

I wrote the first draft of this piece with a number 2 pencil on a legal pad. Did you know there is no 'Spell Cheek' on a legal pad?

Movies

I am not a great movie buff. It is an uncommon year when I have seen three of the five Academy Award-nominated movies. It is even more uncommon that I recognize the name of the supporting actress or actor of the Academy Award winner.

If the movie isn't a comedy or a light-hearted romance with Tom Hanks, Billy Crystal, Nicole Kidman or Ashley Judd, I usually beg off going. For example, I watched Sandra Bullock in Miss Congeniality with my grandson about 12 times and I think I was as eager as he the 12th time.

This year has been an exception. I have seen most of the movies generating Academy Award buzz. I'm not sure why. Maybe it is an unusual year for movies. Maybe I have just become more malleable as I get older. Of one thing I am sure—it is not the price or quality of the popcorn.

Good Night and Good Luck was a fantastic film depicting television journalism in its early days. David Strathairn turns in an Oscar-worthy portrayal of Edward R. Murrow in his historic confrontation with Senator Joseph McCarthy. Murrow shows how it is possible—nay essential—for a courageous newsman, backed by his bosses and armed with facts, to halt a narcissistic, power-drunk government official from devastating and career-ending abuse of people. McCarthy used irresponsible accusations and smear tactics against hundreds of innocent people—even accusing the army of harboring communists—until Murrow held his tactics up to the light of truth.

Another remarkable film released this year is *Capote* with Philip Seymore Hoffman. Whether you have ever read a word of Truman Capote's writings or seen one of his plays is immaterial. You will be overwhelmed with the acting of Hoffman. I was a bit disappointed because I expected the film to be about Capote's life. In fact, it is an exploration, in depth, of his writing *In Cold Blood*, his book about the murder and murderers of a Kansas family, and the subsequent fate of the two killers. Forget the story. Hoffman's performance is worth the price of the movie and the indulgence of bad popcorn.

History of Violence was an accidental thing. As I recall, it was a compromise between something I really wanted to see and something else my wife wanted to see. The film opens with Viggo Mortensen, of *Lord of the Rings* fame, running his small-town diner and enjoying his Norman Rockwell family. His life is turned upside down when he receives a visit from a couple of men claiming to be old friends. After a decidedly unfriendly confrontation, the movie takes a drastic turn and provides an hour and half of great suspense. It is a re-heated serving of Altman, with a healthy dash of Hitchcock.

Joaquin Phoenix and Reece Witherspoon do the most believable Johnny Cash and June Carter Cash one could imagine in *Walk the Line*. The single detraction of *Walk the Line* is that I have seen *Ray* with Jamie Foxx. If I had to describe *Walk the Line* on a bumper sticker, I would say it is *Ray* Lite. But even at that, it is a tour de force for the two actors. Phoenix does his own singing and playing, and it is not a Frank Gorshin kind of imitative performance. It is a Johnny Cash reincarnated kind of performance. Witherspoon does an equally credible June Carter Cash. She and Phoenix have a wonderful chemistry that nails the honesty of the film.

The film that seems to be receiving the most Oscar buzz is also the most controversial. *Brokeback Mountain*, the love story of two gay cowboys, has been lauded for its story, the acting, the directing, and about any other facet of filmmaking one can imagine. If you can forget for a moment that the two lovers in this film are both male, you can appreciate that it is a story of unrequited love, interrupted by the unavoidable and dismal facts of life. Again, the acting is superb. Heath Ledger is my pick to receive the Oscar for Best Actor, for a couple of reasons. First, he is marvelous in the role. Second, it is a groundbreaking performance and Hollywood will see it as the politically correct thing to do. Jake Gyllenhaal may very likely be named Best Supporting Actor for the same reason.

There are other good films out there this year. Two of them are *Crash* (we rented that one) and *The Constant Gardner*. So, if you haven't been to the movie for a while, give yourself an entertainment treat and take in one of the above flicks. Any of them will make you forget how bad the popcorn is.

Clichés

I did a recent column resolving not to make any resolutions this year. Instead I would simply try to practice a few things I would like to make habit. Well, I have changed my mind…sort of. Actually, I'm ready to break my resolution not to make any resolutions. I hereby resolve to refrain from using the most sickening of current clichés.

There are some phrases out there that have served their purpose to the point of becoming meaningless and are indicative of a non-thinker.

The number one worn out cliché is "at the end of the day." OK, it replaced, "when all is said and done," "as this winds down," and perhaps another one or two that escape my memory. It is used by people who know better. News commentators, print reporters, ordinary folks and especially politicians. The mention of politicians "opens up a whole new can of worms." (Forgive me, but it will probably happen again.)

The cliché du jour is "fiscal cliff." There are those who think that "at the end of the day," the "fiscal cliff" is just about as dangerous as the "Wizard of Oz." Not being an economist I can't "speak to that." (Even if I were an economist, I couldn't speak to an inanimate, overused figure of speech.)

On the other hand, there are those who think the "fiscal cliff" is the economic "perfect storm," and that we would be facing a "financial apocalypse" if the "powers that be" can't "come to Jesus" on the issue soon.

What I hope to do in this column is "connect the dots" on the question of clichés. As one stares at a computer screen in an effort to create a readable essay of about 750 words, one realizes this is where "the rubber meets the road." Doing a column, one is frequently challenged to "think outside the box." There are days when I sit at the keyboard and I can "hit the ground running." There are other days when I just can't "see the light at the end of the tunnel."

"Long story short," a writer simply has to "cut to the chase" at times and "give it his/her best shot" and "let the chips fall where they may." "Going forward," we often get lazy and "pick the low-hanging fruit."

Politicians are especially good at creating clichés. They are prone to "throw people under the bus" to "save their own hide." They like to accuse each other of "re-inventing the wheel," and they frequently let us know that "it is what it is." And of course, "read my lips" needs no further explanation. They will often "put a bug in each other's ear." When they are faced with a "doomsday decision," they let us know that they were forced to "drink the Kool Aid."

The only people more prolific at clichés than politicians are athletes and sports figures. "One game at a time" is the only way any sports team ever faces the season. They always "come to play." A good athlete is always a "stud." And there are times when a team "gets in the zone" and has a successful run. It "goes without saying" that you had better bring your "A game" in any athletic endeavor because your opponent is "come to play."

Players often need to "man up" or they will be replaced. We all know that, no matter the game, "it is a game of inches." And, the team that scores first drew "first blood." I could "wrap this thing up" using only sports clichés, but that would "bore you to tears" and I couldn't "bear the thought."

To "put the cherry on top of this little sundae," I am aware, dear reader, that you can think of dozens of "time-worn" phrases that could have and should have "made the cut" in this sarcastic epistle that attempts to "hold a mirror up to us," so that we can see ourselves in the "real world." Actually, "at the end of the day," I just "ran out of steam."

Colloquialism

A few weeks ago, I wrote a column in which I used the term *pig in a poke*. Since that column appeared, several people have asked what's the meaning of *pig in a poke*.

I guess I should explain that a poke, in this instance, is a sack. The column dealt with the presidential race and my point was that no matter the experience, knowledge, or apparent fitness of the candidates, we can't tell what we are getting until they are elected and react to the pressures of the office.

The term is a colloquialism I often heard Aunt Molly use when talking about buying an item sight unseen or hiring someone she did not know. We lived in a rural community where almost everyone farmed, ranched, or made a living off farmers or ranchers. Those expressions were part of our language in those days.

I'll share a few that come to mind and provide a brief explanation of each. For you readers who are over 65, I'll be *preaching to the choir*, but for some of you younger readers, perhaps I can introduce you to a few expressions that will spice up your conversation or your writing.

Too wet to plow is a saying that has nothing to do with the amount of rain that has fallen. Unless, of course, rain has fallen. It means that there might be trouble as a result of some individual's or group's behavior. For instance, if I were late getting home from a date when in high school, I would likely find it *too wet to plow*. If the basketball team played poorly on Friday night, the coach would make it *too wet to plow* at Monday's practice.

If things were going well and we were prospering, or if we had an unusual streak of good luck, we were *in high cotton*. There might not be a stalk of cotton on the place, but the metaphor represented well-being. It no doubt came from the time when cotton was picked or pulled by hand. In a dry year the cotton did not grow very tall and when one had to bend all day to pick the bolls off the shorter stalks, it was much more tedious and tiring. Also, cotton-pickers were paid by the pound and one could pick lots more cotton in the same amount of time when the stalks were tall and loaded with bolls.

A couple colloquialisms that I have not heard since my granddad died in the early '70s are *kicked over the traces* and *spit out the bit*. He was an adult before there were automobiles, of course, and *kicked over the traces* was a reference to an ornery horse that was difficult to harness. Traces are a part of the harness that hitches a horse to a wagon and when the horse was acting up, he might kick at the traces until he freed himself.

Spit out the bit also applies to horses and refers to a run-away. The horse didn't literally *spit out the bit*, but it means one can no longer control the animal with the reins and bit.

So, if Granddad were describing some fellow who might have gotten in trouble with the law and left the country, he might say, "He *kicked over the traces, spit out the bit* and he's not been heard from since."

One should be careful using colloquialisms or metaphors around young children. Until about age 10, kids think quite literally. Once I overheard my mother say that "Lois keeps the house as neat as a pin," referring to a teen-age girl who watched us and helped mother around the house. I told Lois that my mother said she kept the house like a pig pen. My mother spent several days trying to convince Lois that she didn't say that at all and that her son was prone to shoot his mouth off about things he knew nothing about. (I suppose that hasn't changed very much.)

There are a couple of colloquial expressions that I recall from childhood that have a clear meaning, but I have not a clue about their origin. *Light a shuck* means to leave in a hurry. I have no way to connect the statement and the meaning. Corn shucks will burn, but why lighting one would cause someone to leave abruptly is beyond me. *I'll be a monkey's uncle* is another the connection of which escapes me.

It means that one is awed or surprised by a circumstance or event, but what the connection is, I don't know.

A tough row to hoe and *let's head to the barn* are colloquialisms which, like most of those mentioned above, have their origin in the agrarian life of 50 or more years ago. The former, means there is a formidable obstacle ahead and refers to the days when we chopped cotton, or corn and one row was especially full of weeds—or Johnson grass in my case. The other means it's time to quit working in the field and take the horses to the barn. Today, it means it's quitting time.

One of my favorites, often employed by Aunt Molly is, *"I'd know his hide in a tan yard."* That was often her answer to the question, "Do you know (remember) old man Johnson?" "Well, of course, I'd know his hide in a tan yard." That phrase is derived from the days when animal hides were tanned in large numbers and the hide was all one had to identify an animal. I'm sure most of them looked quite similar. So, if you discern a *"hide in a tan yard,"* you knew the animal quite well.

I'm told Eskimos have more than 100 words for snow. Likewise, in west Texas, we had lots of terms for dry. One is *dry as a bone*, from the sun-dried skeletons of sheep or cattle in that semi-arid country, I presume. *Stubborn as a mule* was a common metaphor to refer to an unbending individual, of which there were plenty where I grew up. Otherwise, they would have left after about the third devastating drought.

I'm sure many of you have some favorite colloquialisms or metaphors that are unique to where you grew up. I would love to hear from you and your story (s) concerning them. As a would-be writer, I'm not above stealing to fill these columns.

The columns can be *a tough row to hoe*. Sometimes I feel as if *I'm in high cotton*, but then it turns out to be *too wet to plow* and I just feel like *kicking over the traces* and *spitting out the bit* and *heading for the barn*, but *I'm stubborn as a mule* so I finish them.

New Years Resolutions

How many of you make resolutions for the New Year? Almost all of you—right?

How many of you keep those resolutions throughout the year? Almost none of you—right? I don't make resolutions because like you, I couldn't keep them. Well, I did make a resolution one year that I kept. It was to make no New Year resolutions.

While I make no resolutions, there are a few things I like to do just because it seems the right thing to do.

I make a conscious effort to compliment people on their efforts, no matter what that might be. Waiters, yard men, volunteers, acquaintances, clerks, whoever. This is a very stressful time of year for all of us and no matter the job someone is doing, even if they are just average, they might be doing it with a migraine. I try to keep that in mind all year.

When shopping, grocery store, big box store, coffee shop, restaurant, or dentist office, I park in the first parking spot available. Now, that's a bit of a stretch. I don't park at the end of the parking lot just because that's the first parking space available. But, I don't circle the lot three times, looking for that elusive spot on the front row. A little walking doesn't hurt me. In fact, I don't do enough and this is an opportunity to get exercise. It gets my endorphins flowing and I feel more like being complimentary to the clerk or cashier when I get in the store.

I make it a habit to over tip in restaurants or other appropriate locations. Anyone who is waiting tables or doing some menial task where a tip is traditional is not getting rich. My daughter once worked in a restaurant and the stories she told about the rudeness of customers and the Scrooge-like tips she occasionally received…or not, convinced me that a little extra in that situation goes a long way. It says a lot to the service person. A dollar extra goes a long way with a waiter.

When I meet or greet someone, I try to identify a thing or characteristic about which I can make a complimentary or positive comment. Now, that requires a bit of practice, but it also improves one's memory and it feels as good to you as to the person being complimented. Women's hairdo, earrings, jacket, blouse or necklace are obvious targets. Just look for them and make a positive comment. Be careful about mentioning weight. You should know the person's attitude toward gaining or losing. Men are a bit different. Men *do* things, so ask about his hobby—catch any fish lately? Did you shoot your buck this year? Are you still doing woodwork? You get the picture.

I call my kids once a week. Well, that's not quite true. I don't always call, but with this new gadget I have—it's called a phone, but it does so much more—I often text them because they don't always answer the phone. I guess a phone conversation is "so 2011." I can text, but I don't IM or skype or video or youtube or any of those other esoteric conversational modes.

I try to be patient with telemarketers. Now, that's a long stretch. If it is a real person, I will listen until they say, "We are not selling anything." Of course, they are selling something, or they would not be calling. "We are doing a short survey," will also get me to hang up the phone. If they want my opinion on something, they can read this column. I need all my opinions to fill this white space at which I am presently staring.

I volunteer a few hours a week. There are so many non-profits that depend largely on volunteers for their existence. This town is full of them. You can begin with your church, if you are so inclined. Then there's the food bank, the schools, various shelters, the hospital, hospice, and dozens of other organizations and facilities. There is an organization called RSVP which matches volunteers with jobs that best suits their likes, talents and vocations. It is located in Seguin. Full disclosure. I'm retired and have some time on my hands.

I suppose this column is a bit preachy, and I can hear you now saying, "I don't believe he does all those things all the time." And, you would be right. But I work on it.

If you have already made your resolutions for the New Year, I hope they are realistic and go beyond "losing weight" and "saving money."

Meanwhile, have a Happy and Prosperous New Year. Peace.

Stroll in the Park

After almost two weeks of relative inactivity, I felt a sudden urge to get the body moving and enjoy the crisp air, mellowed by the comforting sun. It was as bright as a yellow rose and as welcoming as a warm bath. My path would lead me through Prospect Park to Hunter Road. It is somewhat primitive along that route and often I am transported to an earlier time of my life when the dry pastures of Concho County were my playground.

As I walk along the mile and a half (approximately) route, I am on the lookout for wildlife. However, as was often the case with my gambols through the pastures of Concho County, my passive search proves futile. I have walked this route many times and searched the woodlines and oak motts for signs of a furry friend. It has proved to be of no avail. I have seen many more deer on Belvin Street and Rogers Ridge than I have encountered in the wilds of the park. When I see my next deer in the park, it will be my first.

On the other hand, the park abounds with glorious flora of all sorts and descriptions. That is a part of what reminds me of the pastures I roamed as a 10 year old. The prickly pear cactus is more than plentiful, and it is preparing to burst forth in full bloom. Seems to me these cacti are like watermelons–red and yellow. Our Prospect Park variety is of the yellow persuasion and the otherwise forbidding clumps will soon explode with numerous butter-colored blooms.

However, I can't fully enjoy those enticing plants in all their glory. Each time I pass one, I am reminded of the time my good friend, Kenneth and I were on the creek bank, smoking a Duke's Mixture when it came time for us to go home. I was barefoot that afternoon and my friend, Kenneth had on shoes. That was not usually the case. Nevertheless, I asked him to carry me piggy-back up the hill and out of a patch of burrs. As we made our way up the rocky slope, Kenneth slipped on a rock and lost his balance. He fell backward instead of forward for a reason that has not yet been explained to me. And, yes, he fell into a clump of prickly pear.

For the sake of simplicity, I will explain that prickly pears have two levels of self-defense. One, I will call spines and the other, I will call stickers. The spine is an inch to an inch an a half long, stiff and needle-like. The sticker is less than a quarter inch long, very flexible and is found in bunches on the cactus leaf. To avoid the tedium of this whole story, I will simply report that I spent several hours on my belly as my mother removed as many of those pesky little things as possible. I spite of her diligence, two weeks later I would still occasionally locate one the stickers as I pulled on a my underwear or a shirt.

Back to the joy of communing with nature on an idyllic Saturday morning. The recent rains, such as they were, have re-carpeted the landscape with lush covers of green. And the trees are pregnant with buds of fresh foliage and latent growth. There is a faint aroma of new life in the air and a sense of renewal.

For bird lovers, familiar songs, gently penetrate and disrupt the surrounding stillness. The ornithological varieties range from the dainty wren and the tuneful mockingbird to the ubiquitous vulture that we call buzzards. I came across a flock of the latter on the edge of the trail and my presence was much less frightening than the carrion was enticing. They hardly gave me a glance in passing.

We are blessed with more than one of these semi-primitive parks. I make the point that the parks are semi-primitive because there are improved trails throughout most of the areas. And, there are benches, constructed of native materials that serve as rest stops or spots for private meditations and reflections. Treat yourself to a morning of low impact exercise, an escape from industrial noise, a concerto of natural music, and a visit to the vultures' cafeteria. It's as easy as a walk in the park.

Cancer

I hope this column does not appear to be too self-serving, in spite of the fact that it is…sort of. It's just that two situations came together in a serendipitous way and a third incident served to meld them into this column.

First, I sat staring at a blank page with a deadline looming. Second, I have recently been diagnosed for the second time with cancer—on a lymph node, this time. The third incident was the receipt of an email from a friend of mine who said, she had been reading my book (Ordinary People: Heroes, Creators, Survivors) and she listed a few profiles she had read.

That caused me to retrieve my own copy of the book and thumb through the volume, vividly remembering most of the interviews. Suddenly, I was struck by the number of people about whom I wrote that were cancer survivors.

This column is aimed at those who have cancer, have survived cancer and may be likely to get cancer. Of course, it is largely warmed-over prose, but I have no pride when it comes to filling the white space of a newspaper.

To set the scene, I'll start with my own cancer experience. I had been going to my urologist for a couple of visits to get prescriptions for prostate issues. Things were going so well, I was about to cancel my June 24, 2009 appointment. A friend convinced me to keep the appointment. The doctor had told me he was going to scope my bladder to see if I had stones that might be causing my trouble.

He inserted his scope, looked around inside my bladder, mumbled a few uums, uhhs, uh-hus and finally raised up, looked me in the eye and said, "Bibb, the good news is you have no stones. The bad news is you have cancer." Before I could respond, he turned to his nurse and said, "Clear my appointments for the day, we are doing surgery this afternoon."

By 4:00 p.m., I was out of the surgical center, and at 7:00 p.m., I attended a dinner party. Three days later, I left San Marcos for two and a half months in Colorado where I cycled, hiked 12,000 feet peaks, and just generally acted as if nothing happened. No chemo. No radiation. It was quick, clean, relatively painless, and did not interfere with my life at all. I never thought of myself as a cancer survivor.

That same doctor enrolled me in a study at MD Anderson Cancer Center in Houston and for the past three and a half years, I have been seen, scoped, scanned, and scored by the finest oncologists in the world. Came out clean every time. Until January 16, 2013. The scan revealed an "unspecified enlargement of a lymph node in the pelvic region." February 1, 2013, a biopsy of that lymph node revealed cancer. So, now, we are up to date.

Back to the book. As noted above, I marvel at the number of cancer survivors I interviewed for that modest volume.

I'll begin with one of the more unusual cases I encountered. Laura Pratt began the interview with "Sometimes I pass a mirror and catch a glimpse of my body and I do a slight double-take. I don't look like everyone else. That is about the only time I am aware that I have only one arm."

Laura continues, "When I was in first grade, we noticed that my right arm would not straighten completely." After going to doctors all over north central Texas Laura was finally referred to a surgeon in Fort Worth, by a friend's orthodontist. The surgeon found the tumor, identified as *synovial sarcoma* in the ligament of the elbow joint. It was a rare case because that particular tumor is normally found in the elderly and Laura was only nine years old.

At M.D. Anderson Cancer Center in Houston the decision was made to amputate Laura's arm. Her reaction to that news was, "Nine year olds are bullet proof…I didn't really believe they were going to take off my arm until I awoke from surgery."

At the time of the interview, Laura had two daughters, six and three and she explained a number of ways in which she has improvised and compensated as a result of having lost an arm. She is, indeed, a survivor and a healthy one.

Another story of survival involves a mother and a daughter. After feeling bad for about a year, from 1986 to 1987, with no doctors able to detect a problem, Janette Ramsay finally went to a psychiatrist and asked, "Could all this be in my head?" He scheduled a battery of tests which showed very low counts for cancer indicators. However, she was scheduled for surgery during which, the doctor discovered her perilous condition. He removed 85 percent of her colon, 27 lymph nodes and discharged her with the not too jolly prognosis that she had a five percent chance to live six months.

At the insistence of her mother, she got a second opinion. This time she was told there was nothing that could be done and she would not live a year anyway. According to Janette, "That's the first time I really heard what I was being told."

Janette's daughter Jan Stark describes her first awareness of a problem: "I was having lunch with a recruit we were courting for the law firm (Jan was practicing law with a major firm in Dallas). I was talking and all of a sudden no words came out. I felt so weird. I almost wrote on a napkin, 'Take me to the hospital.'"

The first doctor Jan saw thought she might be suffering from a seizure disorder and ordered a CAT scan. A brain tumor showed up on the scan. Surgery ensued and it was discovered she had primary brain cancer.

These three individuals are cancer survivors. Full disclosure: Jan Stark is largely disabled by her brain cancer, but is still struggling to defeat it.

My book was not meant to be a paean to cancer survivors. Rather, I simply wanted to put together in compact form a tableau of the people of San Marcos and Hays County. Nevertheless, there are profiles which will encourage and inspire you if you or someone close to you is suffering from, being treated for, or has survived cancer.

You can begin with Jerry Supple's story. Most will recognize that he was president of *Southwest Texas State* until his efforts changed the name to *Texas State*. Jerry survived seven years after his initial diagnosis and continued in his post as president for a number of years, during which he was an extremely competitive tennis player and golfer.

Cornelia Cheatham is a foster parent who has mothered an untold number of children. Her career in fostering began as a result of a diagnosis of breast cancer. According to Cornelia,"…if I could go through six months of chemo, I could do anything," and, inspired by a television show, she and her husband joined the program several years ago. Recently, one of her foster children recognized my name from the profile I wrote about Cornelia and in our conversation, I learned that she now has six girls in her home.

Other cancer survivors whose stories appear in the book are: Kathy Morris, our former mayor, Virginia Witte, Jim Wacker, and John Ferguson, Jr.

Not all are still with us, but I call them survivors for what they accomplished after their diagnosis. And all their stories are inspirational for anyone facing the Big C.

For the reasons I have enumerated, I expect you may have to suffer this column when the inspiration strikes for the next 10-15 years.

Valentine's Day

It is February, the month to remember Saint Valentine with cards, candy, love notes and special gifts to the one we love. Romance is definitely in the air—well in the wild at any rate. How do I know this? On each of my recent bike rides I have counted at least six dead polecats on the roads on which I ride. So, it has to be the season when skunks are called to propagate the world with more skunks. The call of love is so great the cute little black and white striped mammal will risk (and often lose) his life to find the perfect mate. It is romance time in Polecat world.

Humans, perhaps with greater caution, but no less desire will engage in similar acts to initiate or renew the flame of love. In searching for more information on Valentine's Day, I found that the origin is quite murky. There was a Saint Valentine or maybe two.

One reference states, "Saint Valentine, was a widely recognized third century Roman saint commemorated on February 14 and associated since the High Middle Ages with a tradition of courtly love." The reference goes on to say, "Nothing is known reliably...except his name and the fact that he died on the Via Flaminia, north of Rome on February 14."

Since he is reported to have died on a road, I can't help relating his death to the numerous little skunks I have encountered on my bike rides. I wonder if his motivation was the same as the skunks. Let's hope, for the sake of love, Saint Valentine's death was a more dignified occurrence than that of our little mammals crossing the road as they respond to their irresistible, instinctive urges.

Whatever the origin of Valentine's Day, it has become another marketing bonanza for the flowers, candy and restaurant business. According to one source, 58 million pounds of chocolate will be bought at a cost of $1.5 billion. Flowers will bring in $1.8 billion and $3.5 billion will be spent on prix fixe dinners. I couldn't find the dollar value of cards, but Hallmark has more than 1,400 Valentine designs.

I would suppose that the only holiday on which more candy is sold and consumed is Halloween. I don't have figures for that, but seems I have read that it is the biggest day of the year for candy sales.

Do the elementary schools still celebrate Valentine's Day as we once did? In the lower grades—probably first through fourth—I remember Valentine's Day as the time when room mothers brought cookies and hot chocolate to school. Mrs. Bryson (she was my teacher for three of those four years) put a box at the back of the room and we students brought our valentines for our class mates. We dropped them in the box and after the hot chocolate and cookies, we passed out the Valentines. The excitement of handing out the cards was the highlight of the day.

I suppose we were supposed to have a card for each classmate, but it didn't always work that way. The popular kids got more valentines than others. I was interested in just one card. I was concerned only with getting a card from Noelene (yep, that was her name, God rest her soul) Williams and what that card had to say.

I suppose it is a good thing that we have a day set aside for love. We have days to honor about everything else. We have National Cookies Day, National Secretaries Day, National Dairy Cow Day, National Eat Beef Day, National Eat Cheese Day and National Bicycle Day. (I made up the last three, but I bet they exist.)

I think we should name February as National Polecats Roadkill Month. February can use a few more commemorations. My source only lists two for February. It is Black History month and Career and Technical Education month. April has seven commemorations. That just doesn't seem fair, even if February is the shortest month.

If you are a movie buff and movies are a major source of your romantic life, here are the top five romantic movies of all time. This list comes from Google, my source for avoiding real research. The movies listed by that infallible web site are: *The Notebook, Titanic, Pretty Woman, When Harry Met Sally,* and *Ghost.* I have not seen *The Notebook* or *Titanic,* but I assure you *Pretty Woman, When Harry Met Sally,* and *Ghost* are indeed lightweight romances that entertain and, in the right setting, might even inspire.

So, if expensive jewelry, a gourmet dinner, and Godiva chocolates are out of your pocketbook range, rent a movie, impress on your lover that Valentine's Day is that time of year when procreation is a really popular activity, at least among Polecats, and hope for a romantic interlude.

The Bus Ride

She is a trim, handsome lady whose neat gray hair frames her friendly smile as she welcomes me aboard her 48 passenger school bus. Joanie Graves drives bus number 46 for the San Marcos Consolidated Independent School District (SMCISD). It is one of 74 that will leave the bus barn today around 2:45 PM to return students from school to their homes. I will be on that bus. More than 50 years have passed since I was on such a trip.

The last time I was on a bus remotely resembling this one, I was a senior in high school. The good new is I sat next to Jamesina Fowler, holding hands. The bad news is she got off at the first stop.

My ride today is the result of my accepting Oscar Harell's invitation to the San Marcos Transportation Advisory Board to visit his bus barn and accompany one of his drivers on a route. Oscar is SMCISD, Director of Transportation.

Following Oscar's instructions, I arrived at the facility at Wonder World Drive and IH 35 at 2:00 PM. Oscar has been in his present job about two years and is proud of the job his people do getting 5,271 students to and from seven schools five days a week. He is eager to show me how it is done.

First, he takes me on a tour of the facility. During the walk through, he casually mentions that when he arrived two and a half years ago, the transportation department was $300,000.00 in the red. It is now operating within budget. If that isn't astounding enough, he pointed out that he keeps 74 buses on the road with only three mechanics.

With that sort of staff, I began looking for a wrecker to retrieve stranded vehicles. I was informed that SMCISD Transportation does not own such a vehicle. Oscar pointed out a pick-up truck outfitted with tool boxes along both sides of the cargo compartment. "That's my retrieval vehicle he said. And we only call a commercial wrecker about once a year.

"I don't need a wrecker, but I need maintenance bays that cover the length of the bus so that my drivers and mechanics can service buses during wet weather." Oscar rattles off a litany of shop practices he has implemented since his arrival and takes care to introduce me to everyone we meet. Al is putting four new tires on a bus. Pat is a mechanic who also drives a bus, and today he is repairing a leak in the roof of one.

Mario is on a 12 foot aluminum ladder, working with Pat, trying to repair the leak. Oscar points out, "Mario is our welder. He has experience welding on offshore oil rigs.

Some of the ladies used to work with commercial upholstery, and they do all our upholstery repair. I save about two-thirds the cost of going outside to get that sort of work done." Economy.

I inquired about a metal bar across the front of the bus. Oscar put me in the driver's seat and with the aid of one of his staff demonstrated how the bar swings out when the bus is stopped, forcing the departing children to walk several feet away from the bus so that they can easily be seen. Safety.

He then puts me in a seat and explains that his buses are not required to have seat belts because the seat backs are padded and are higher than my line of vision. I will learn later that this feature has a collateral advantage to the driver. Each bus also has a seating chart. Safety/control.

Next, I meet Rick, shop foreman, who gives me 12 reasons why the shop needs a vehicle lift bay. His pitch is sincere and convincing. Next, I meet Richard. He checks all the fluids in every bus every day to relieve the mechanics of that tedious task. He also changes burned out lights. *All the fluids of every bus every day!* Can you believe it? Attention to detail.

Oscar then shows me the driver's break room. It must accommodate 80 people. I have seen larger clothes closets. Four people occupy the room and when one decides to leave, two of the occupants move to allow him egress. If six people occupied the room at once, I'm sure they would be violating the fire code. Then, he shows me the restrooms. To say that the facilities are limited, is...well, DUH! Yet, morale is high. Leadership.

I meet a few drivers. Lupe has been driving 19 years; Mary is a four year veteran. Then Oscar shows me his office. It is about the size of a port-a-pottie. He shares the inconveniences of restricted space. Leadership.

Randy is in charge of the daily operations. He makes sure every bus gets out on time on the right route with a driver. Moe is a driver who trains new drivers. Lisa coordinates all transportation for special populations, pre-k, and alternative programs. Fred plans transportation for all the field trips, football games and special events. Each of these people drives a regular route every day. Economy/versatility.

Finally, I am put in Joanie Graves' charge. She does a thorough check of her bus–lights, tires, doors, outside, underside, and inside. Joanie describes her job: "It is a perfect job for me. I have seven grandchildren, six are small, so it gives me lots of time with them. I don't work during the summer. I love it, I love driving." Safety/morale.

At 2:40 PM, we pulled out of the busy parking lot and headed for Crockett Elementary. The first stop, was for an 85 car train as it passed along the tracks in the vicinity of Widelite. With the street repair projects on the southwest side of town, we took a circuitous route, to reach our destination.

At Crockett, Joanie informs me, "The kids we are picking up now are kindergarten through fourth grade. They have to be delivered to a parent or a responsible adult. We have to know what's going on or we don't let them off the bus. We also walk the younger ones across the street. They can only get off at their designated stop. If they are going home with someone, they must have a written form from the school office."

Forty-eight kids begin boarding the bus. The decibel level is equal to 12 B-52's taking off. Joanie greeted every kid by name and checked that he/she was sitting in the proper seat. Sitting is the operative word, here. The bus doesn't move until she is satisfied that all her kids are properly seated. Safety/control.

We begin a winding trip through San Marcos, like a corpuscle coursing its way through a human's veins and arteries. Franklin Street to RR 12, down Sarah to Coers Circle for our first stop. Joanie opens the door and waits to see a parent appear in the doorway of the house before dropping the student. This routine will be repeated for the next hour and a half until all 40+ kids are delivered. Concern/safety.

I look toward the back of the bus and no heads are visible. The high seat backs aid Joanie in controlling the kids because it provides a certain level of separation. Control of the children is a major contributor to safety. At RR 12 and Hutchison (Palmer's), she kills the engine, dismounts and takes the hand of two students as she walks them across the street. Safety.

I was shocked by the size of the backpacks these youngsters carry. Many of them stretch from the student's shoulders to the bend of the knees. What do they carry that requires such a large pack. My rucksack in Viet Nam was not that big.

The route is difficult because the bus is required to negotiate so many sharp corners. Many auto drivers ignore the bus's need for extra room. So Joanie waits. Caution.

This route covers San Marcos from Franklin Street to Hutchison, Hopkins, Riverside, Cheatham, Sycamore, Field and the Barbara Street area. Joanie is in and out the bus, taking kids across the street. She makes sure someone meets every child. Security/safety.

When the bus is empty, we head for Hernandez Intermediate School where we pick up 20 or so kids, then we make a stop at Goodnight Junior High. Finally, we make a pick up at San Marcos High. An hour later, all those kids have been delivered along a route similar to the one we followed to deliver the elementary school kids.

After almost three hours, we head back to the bus barn. Ninety or so kids have found their way home safely, thanks to a tightly knit, smooth working, overachieving team with extremely high morale... especially one tough, concerned and caring Grandma.

Women's Center

So, how was your Mother's Day? Most mothers will be honored in some way today. Your unique place in the world will be recognized and you will be told, in a variety of ways—breakfast in bed, a special meal, flowers, a gift, a grown child's visit—that you are special. You will be recognized as the family focal point. You will be held up as the hub of a civilized society. And the hope is that you will feel special.

The majority of mothers will be especially proud today. They will exalt in their accomplishments and the accomplishments of their children. However, as you read this, there are mothers who are looking for only one thing, safety—for themselves and their children.

After prolonged battering, psychological abuse, sexual abuse, and intimidation, many women feel anything, but special. Years of living with household violence will often drive a woman to desperation. When that desperation drives a woman to action, there is one place she can be assured of finding safety, the Hays-Caldwell Women's Center.

Elva Gonzalez who heads the Family Violence Outreach Team has been with the Center probably longer than any other staff member. She began as a part-time employee in 1979 while a student at Southwest Texas State University. "I work with battered women to get protective orders and legal aid assistance," says Elva. "I give them information about their rights and options. I help them understand the legal system and how it affects them. I insure they are telling their lawyers what they need to tell them and that they get through the legal system with the protection they need."

Responding to my question, Elva informed that there is no typical battered woman. She said the victim might be any age with any level of affluence, and any number of children. A large number of clients are in their thirties with two to three children. Again, the children fit no mold. They range in age from newborn to late teens. While it is difficult to define the typical client of the center, there is one commonality that is almost always present. The battering has been happening a lot and has been happening for many years.

Elva says, "Usually, they have tried other options. Going to their parents, separating, leaving the batterer, asking him to go to counseling, going to their minister. But the abuse is escalating and the victim is really, really afraid."

Janet Burke, a shy, somewhat reticent woman confirms that the women are afraid and desperate. A mother of five grown children, she once sought refuge in just such a place as the one she now oversees as the Shelter Services Director.

"We provide them safety," Janet responded when asked what her staff does for the women. "We provide counseling for the women. And for the children. We help them with whatever issue they may be working on–legal, family issue, school, whatever."

I suggested it might be like a huge family. "Lots of huge families," Janet responded. "I put my own family aside when I'm at work, and I try to put the shelter families aside when I go home to my family. While they are here, they are in total control of what they want. The families decide what their goals will be and we try to help them reach those goals.

"We work a lot on self-esteem. Typically, when a woman first comes here, she feels unworthy, totally inadequate, and can't make decisions. She has no idea what to do. She's tired of being hit and she's tired of being used as an object. She has come here to make things better and we try to help her. We provide support groups, we let her know she is worthy and that she is capable. We do this by supporting the decisions she makes. We may offer suggestions, but we refuse to make any decisions for her."

Janet pointed out that having a number of families in the shelter is an advantage. They work with each other. They support and encourage each other. She says many of the families have been isolated and have had little interaction with others. In addition, many of the people who work in the shelter have been abused. As in Janet's case, it was her experience in a shelter that drew her to her present work.

"The people who have been through the battering experience can relate," Janet emphasizes, "because the clients know that you know what they are going through."

I asked Janet to describe the worst case she has seen. "I have seen a lot of bad cases. But I can't answer that question because I see a lot of physical abuse, and I see a lot of psychological and emotional abuse and to me, one is just as damaging as the other. People respond differently. To the woman who comes in here, her case is the worst case. I have seen cases involving murder, I have seen cases involving extreme psychological abuse. Every case is unique."

The staff of the Women's Center lives by that credo. It is impossible to get them to categorize or generalize. Every person who enters the center has individual needs, a unique attitude, and personal expectations. The staff is trained to recognize this aspect of their clients and to emphasize it. This attitude goes a long way toward restoring a person's sense of self and individual worthiness.

As an example of a grotesque case, another member of the staff related the story of a woman whose husband put her in a barrel-like barbecue grill over hot coals. The woman's mother, who was bed-ridden, climbed out of bed, managed to get a gun, crawled outside and stopped the torture by threatening to shoot him. Her daughter managed to escape with major burns and injuries. She found refuge at the Women's Center.

"I know of at least seven women, once clients of the shelter, who have been killed by their batterers in the past nine years," volunteered Janet. Marla Johnson, Executive Director of the Center went on to say that seldom is the batterer convicted of murder. In fact, she knew of no case in which that happened.

Ruthann Gordon, Director of Administrative Services, when asked how she came to her present job, replied, "I was just led to be here. I was looking for a job and as I scanned the paper, it just jumped out at me. The ad said Hays-Caldwell Women's Center needs receptionist. I called and said, 'I'm supposed to be there.' Elva and two other people interviewed me and I didn't look any further. I knew I was supposed to be here. I called every day to see if I got the job. Finally, they called and said I didn't get the job. I said I didn't understand it because God told me I was supposed to have this job."

Elva said, "This lady was really, really serious. I thought, if God told her she was supposed to have this job, maybe we need to look at her again."

"It paid about $7,000.00 a year," according to Ruthann. "It definitely wasn't the money."

Ruthann's attitude is typical of the staff. Marla Johnson had aspirations of becoming a Certified Public Accountant. With an MBA from Southwest Texas, she discovered she did not care for that sort of work. A friend told her there might be a job at the Women's Center. Ruthann answered the phone when Marla called. Marla asked about openings. Ruthann informed her they were looking for an Executive Director, but before she would elaborate, she wanted to know Marla's age. When told she was 35, Ruthann decided she might be a legitimate candidate. Prior to Marla's arrival, there was significant turbulence in the leadership of the Center. Marla says she feels as though she was dropped into the job from outer space. She says she cried every single day for two years as she felt totally inadequate to the task. "But," she says, "the people in this room (Janet, Elva, and Ruthann) got me through it and I finally began to understand I could do it."

What is the best part of working with the Center? Elva Gonzalez responded, "Seeing the women come in feeling doubt, afraid, hopeless." At this point, her voice began to choke and tears filled her eyes as she continued, "and watching them leave happy and putting their life back together and just having a better life. Seeing how just a little help makes such a difference." At this point all four women and the interviewer were reaching for tissue or handkerchiefs.

Hays-Caldwell Women's Center is a private, non-profit corporation which serves a desperate population. They are funded by grants, donations and fund raisers. This Mother's Day as you are enjoying the peace and blessings of a close and loving family, remember the families whose greatest blessing is that they are they are out of danger; they are safe at the Hays-Caldwell Women's Center.

Salvation Army Bell Ringer

One of the best TV commercials I have seen in a long while is running during this Christmas season. It is a public service announcement (PSA). Some PSAs are quite good because the Advertising Council cooperates in making them. Some are terrible because they look as if they were made with someone's hand-held 8 mm camera in someone else's kitchen.

The commercial to which I refer is the Salvation Army ad which depicts a homeless man searching for a place to sleep; the aftermath of a natural disaster showing people being rescued from a flood; an addict passed out in a tenement; and survivors of a fire who have lost everything. Each scene depicts a situation of extreme loss or despair that evokes in the viewer the feeling of, "But for the Grace of God, that could be me." Unobtrusively and without fanfare a Salvation Army bell ringer appears in each scene. No voice-over; no plea for donations; no hard sell. Just a Salvation Army bell ringer.

It is a powerful message that says, "The Salvation Army is always there."

Last week, I had the privilege of being a Salvation Army bell ringer. Adorned with a Santa cap and a red apron, I stood beside the red kettle from 6:00 p.m. to 8:00 p.m. outside the San Marcos Wal-Mart, and rang my bell. It is the policy of the Salvation Army, as in the commercial, to refrain from verbally soliciting contributions. That was the hardest part of the whole evening for me. (When we go to the grocery store together, my wife frequently asks if I'm running for office because of my propensity to speak to everyone I see.)

I used the term "privilege" earlier because it was my pleasure to observe the people who passed through the doors of the store. Seeing their reaction to me was a valuable experience.

Apparently, it was a busy part of the day, for there seemed to be a steady stream of people going in and out the store. What struck me first was that everyone seemed to be in a hurry. I mean—young, old, tall, short, no matter—there was a look of urgency among all of them. What could be so critical about getting whatever they came for? Maybe that's a pervasive attitude today. It seems everyone is in a hurry; however, when they looked at me, many slowed just a step and most gave me a smile and a nod of appreciation for what I was doing. A few even said, "Bless you."

One of the wonderful things I learned from my two hour stint as a bell-ringer was that we live among generous people. I would estimate that more than half the people who passed by dropped a dollar bill (or more) or a handful of loose change in the kettle.

Many people entering the store searched through their wallet and, finding nothing to contribute, assured me they would have something on the way out. And they did.

Often, parents with small children gave the kids the money to put in the kettle. I was reassured that kids are learning to share.

Young people dressed in the skate-boarder fashion, i.e., skewed baseball cap, low slung pants and Chuck Taylor tennis shoes, donated. (Don't judge a mind/attitude by the adornment on the body.) Texas State students dropped a dollar or two in the kettle. Most who gave were not in the upper income brackets.

I have no idea how much money was collected, but at the end of my tour, the kettle was full. People had trouble pushing their dollar bills into the slot. There is something about giving that makes us all feel a little better. It was a great pleasure to be a part of that generosity. The financial world may be falling apart, but the average American, if that's the guy/gal in work clothes who hurries in and out of Wal-Mart, just before or just after the dinner hour, still has that sense of sharing with his/her neighbor and helping those less fortunate. And, there is always someone less fortunate.

I admit, my feet got a little tired and my knees a little achy, but there was a spring in my step and a new sense of worth when I took off my apron and secured the kettle.

Tourist Information Center

This town is full of volunteers. Lots of retired folks here who contribute selflessly of their time and energy to make this place work. There are facilities that would cease to function or would function at a much reduced level without the effort of volunteers. Some of those facilities or organizations include the food bank, the park system, the Heritage Association, Southside Community Center, Salvation Army, the women's shelter and the numerous others I have not mentioned. One not yet mentioned is the Tourist Information Center (TIC). I plan to expand on that for the next few paragraphs.

I volunteer there twice a month on Wednesday afternoons. It is more fun than work and is quite enjoyable for a glad-hander such as I. People from all over the world pass through the portals of 617 IH 35 South. A part of the Visitor's Bureau under the overall umbrella of the San Marcos Chamber of Commerce, the Tourist Information Center serves a diverse group of people.

Before I became involved with the TIC, I had no idea of the number and types of people who traverse IH-35 and decide to drop in on us for any number of reasons. We get people from Canada, Mexico, Germany, Switzerland, Poland, Luling, Lockhart, Wimberley, Killeen, India, Houston, Minnesota, Colorado, New York, Martindale, California, and North Carolina. In December, there were visitors from 27 states and 10 foreign countries.

Of course, we are on the Snowbird route from the tundra of Minnesota to the tropical Rio Grande Valley, so we get those seeking warmth in Texas' friendly environs south of San Antonio. Many of those visitors have made the trip several times and are familiar with our area. Frequently, they just want to use the bathroom and pick up a new Texas map.

We get people from Dallas, Wichita Falls and Corpus Christi who want to know if Aquarena Springs is still in existence. When told the glass-bottom boats are still running, many ask for directions. There are those from Shreveport, Midland and Fredericksburg who are looking for the Outlet Malls.

They come looking for brochures and maps about San Antonio, Austin, the Hill Country, Natural Bridge Caverns, and the Alamo. Much to my dismay, I recently discovered we do not have brochures about the Alamo. I understand it is the most popular tourist destination in Texas, but the Daughters of the Republic of Texas have not furnished the TIC with a brochure.

A frequently asked question (FAQ in today's tech jargon) is 'what's there to do in San Marcos?' I like that question because it gives me a chance to expound on Wonder Cave, Dick's Classic Garage, the LBJ Museum, Texas Music Theater, our historic district and the many historic buildings, the Alkek Library, Embassy Suites and, of course, the Outlet Malls.

As mentioned, people come to the TIC from all over. With just a little encouragement, I have found that most are willing to talk about their place of origin, their trip, and other subjects of some interest to a casual listener. Others, however, after being cooped up with their spouse and radio static for several hours, are eager to talk about their children, grandchildren, hobbies, spouses, pets and current ailments. So, be careful what you ask for when dealing with road-weary strangers.

The TIC receives calls and visits from people relocating to San Marcos for one reason or another. Most have already found their abode, permanent or temporary, and just want to know more about the area. In addition to providing a verbal tour of the city, i.e., restaurants, churches, the hospital, etc., we let them know about Kyle, Buda, Wimberley, and other places around the county. We also include our neighbors in Comal and Caldwell counties, such as Gruene (music), Lockhart (BBQ) and New Braunfels (German culture).

The TIC is stocked with a plethora of information about the entire Hill Country. The uninitiated would be amazed at the number of brochures, pamphlets and maps available. An example of what I mean is one little brochure, titled Dine In. Go Out. A Dining and Entertainment Guide. There are more restaurants bistros and bars listed in this little information sheet than you could visit in a year. So, as you and your spouse, discuss where to go for dinner or a romantic interlude of drinks and conversation, this little guide will get you just where you want to be.

There are times, of course, when it is very quiet at the TIC. Sitting behind the receptionist's desk, one looks out on the parade of automobiles and trucks on IH 35 and first thing you know you are hypnotized by the constant stream of traffic.

Busy or hypnotic, my days at the TIC are always fun. You never know when a family of East Indians, Belgians, British or a lady from Wimberley will walk through the door with an intriguing story or an interesting question. Of course, there are those who just want to use the bathroom.

Race & Gender

*I have a dream that my four little children will one day
live in a nation where they will not be judged by the color
of their skin, but by the content of their character.*

-Martin Luther King Jr. from the I Have a Dream speech,
delivered August 18, 1963 in Washington, D.C.

The foregoing is one of the most oft quoted excerpts from Dr. King's famous I Have a Dream speech. There are times when I reflect on that priceless piece of rhetoric and ask myself, how close are we to that day? In light of the ongoing presidential primaries, I have been asking myself that question a lot.

As I write this, the South Carolina Democratic primary has just concluded. Barack Obama received 55 percent of the almost 500,000 votes cast. No matter which newscast one listens to this fact is never reported without the follow-on that he received around 80 percent of the African-American vote.

I realize that political junkies and talking-heads like to dissect every tiny aspect of a given election. One ill-informed, so-called newscaster when reporting this fact, added, "I think he only received 10 percent or less of the white vote." (It was 24 percent.) As a pathological optimist, I suppose I'm looking for the Utopian condition where we judge our politicians in the manner Dr. King dreamed that we might judge his children—by the content of their character. And their leadership ability. And their ability to inspire. And their vision for the people and the nation.

Likewise, every time, Senator Clinton's numbers are reported, there seems to be a need to elaborate on the percentage of women who voted for her, as if that might forecast her fitness to be the next president of the United States.

The Republicans do not seem to have this problem, in that all their candidates are white males. Oh, there is the occasional reference to the "evangelical" Christian vote, whatever that is, for Governor Huckabee. And, in fairness, we do have to mention that the talking heads, the analysts, and the other experts often raise the question of whether America can vote for a Mormon such as Mitt Romney. That has received less attention since his speech on the subject.

I understand that Obama and Clinton are history-making candidates. I understand the uniqueness of their circumstances. But, back to my pathological optimism, I wish we had a lot more discussion of their ideas for the future of the country and less about their race and gender.

When Jim Clyburn, the House of Representatives Majority Whip, was asked how black voters would interpret the South Carolina Democratic primary results, he responded, "The same way white people are interpreting it. Here's a guy who gives me hope; he's a guy of the future."

It was about this time last year when the sports pages were full of Super Bowl hype. And almost every story, no matter the writer or the publication, made mention of the fact that it would be a historic game because it was the first time there were two African-American head coaches in the game. For that matter, it was the first time there was at least *one* African-American head coach in the game.

This takes me back to the time when Doug Williams won Super Bowl XXII and was the game's MVP at quarterback for the Washington Redskins. He was one of the few black quarterbacks in the league at the time and it got a lot of attention—like, *can you believe it*? Nowadays, there are a number of black quarterbacks and they get the same praise or criticism as their white counterparts.

The point of all this is that we are far from colorblind or free of gender bias in this country. Martin asked us to judge people by their character, rather than the color of their skin. And, we have come a long, long way, but no matter that Doug Williams was voted MVP, or that Tony Dungy and Lovie Smith took teams to the Super Bowl, or that Barack Obama's inspirational oratory gives us hope, or that Hillary Clinton wows us with her toughness and determination, there is always a modifier before or after their names.

I would like to see the media focus on the real issues of our political contests: poverty, education, immigration, taxes, prejudice and health care.

It is now almost 43 years since Dr. King moved the nation with the resounding revelation of his dream. Do you think it will be another 43 years before there is a Hispanic running against an African-American presidential candidate? Will it take that long before we have a Jewish candidate opposed by a Catholic? How long will it be before a Democrat and a Republican, both women, vie for the presidency of the United States? And, in case it ever happens, will we have outgrown the need to focus on race, religion or gender?

Debates—2008

As I write this (Wednesday morning), I am pondering last night's debate between Hillary and Barack. We're not really on a first name basis, but you know who I mean. I am trying to divine some purpose for these debates other than filling about 3 hours that would otherwise be filled with talkingheads and commercials for Cialis.

The most renowned debates in our national history—the ones we studied in school—the Lincoln-Douglas debates bore little resemblance to the televised dog and pony shows we see today.

In 1858, as they vied for the Senate seat from Illinois, the lesser known Lincoln challenged the well known incumbent, Stephen A. Douglas, to campaign with him so that they might debate the issues of the day. Realizing he had little to gain from the debates Douglas was reluctant, at first, but finally conceded.

What I find so remarkable and, certainly, so different from the televised exhibitions we witness today, are the rules of debate the contestants adhered to. There were seven debates and each followed the same rules. The first contestant spoke for an hour, followed by a one-and-a-half-hour response. The first speaker then had a half-hour rebuttal.

From Doris Kearns Goodwin's *Team of Rivals*: "The huge crowds were riveted for the full three hours, often interjecting comments, cheering for their champion, bemoaning the jabs of his opponent. Newspaper stenographers worked diligently to take down every word, and their transcripts were swiftly dispatched throughout the country."

What is not so different today from 1858 is the slanted coverage the newspapers gave to the debates. Depending on the political bent of the particular paper, the outcome varied widely.

Again from *Team of Rivals:* "At the end of the first debate, the Republican *Chicago Press and Tribune* reported that Mr. Lincoln… was seized by the multitude and borne off on their shoulders, in the center of the crowd of five thousand…with a band of music in front." Observing the same occasion, the Democratic *Chicago Times* claimed that when it was over, Douglas's "excoriation of Lincoln" had been so successful and "so severe, that the republicans hung their heads in shame."

This current series of debates began with nine Republicans and eight Democrats in the race. It reminded me of nothing so much as the Westminster Kennel Club Dog show in Madison Square Garden. All these breeds and varieties—pro v. anti immigration; pro v. anti Iraq war; ideologue v. policy wonk; experience v. novice; national figure v. fringe hanger-on, etc. etc. The so-called debate was covered like a beauty pageant. The line-up was asked a series of largely inane questions, which the candidate largely ignored to make a case for his favorite issue: immigration, corporate greed, abortion, defense, taxes or whatever.

The news coverage reported primarily on the style of each candidate because there was hardly any substance. Had there been I doubt it would have been reported. Some candidates were virtually ignored. Chris Dodd, Sam Brownback—who?—Ron Paul, Mike Gravel and others were seldom asked about anything. Certainly, they were never given an hour to make a presentation.

As the candidates dropped out and the field in each party narrowed to two, the debates have become somewhat more substantive, but to refer to the show as a debate does a disservice to a whole multitude of high school history/English teachers who are at this moment coaching a bunch of teenagers to time their presentations precisely, rebut with facts and citations, and speak extemporaneously.

The current display we refer to as a debate has been labeled by one scribe as a joint interview. Debate or joint interview may be academic. This last one between Hillary and Barack was in the same time slot as American Idol. So, did anyone see it?

From *Team of Rivals:* "…the country people began to stream into town for the great meeting…on foot, on horseback, in buggies, or farm wagons...singly and in small parties of men and women and even children. It was indeed the whole American people that listened to those debates."

Goodwin quotes Lincoln, again in *Team of Rivals*, "The debates [are] the successive acts of a drama...to be enacted not merely in the face of audiences like this, but in the face of the nation."

What do you suppose Lincoln would call the 20 or so debates of the past few months?

Why I Support Obama

This political season has been unusually interesting. Much of it is boilerplate stuff. You know, the rhetoric of politics—experience; voting records; pro-this; anti-that; sound bite, after sound bite. But, as it has shaken out over the last few months, there have been some fascinating developments.

On the Republican side, the contenders were whittled down to a war-hero senator who was practically disowned by the party in 2000. The Democrats, meanwhile, have two history-making contenders whose efforts, coupled with fate, have brought them to this juncture, unfortunately, at the same time.

No need to belabor the fact that Hillary and Barack bring unique aspects of race and gender to the contest. There will be some who support neither because of those characteristics. There will be some who support one or the other simply because of those characteristics.

Me? I'm supporting Obama for several reasons, but the principal reason I support him is what he has done for me and what he will do for me. Now, that is not quite as crass as it sounds. I'll explain later.

A little personal history. I grew up in rural west Texas. Farmers, ranchers, close neighbors, Baptists, Church of Christ, Caucasian, Anglo-Saxon. Ford, Chevrolet, Farmall and John Deere. Cotton, milo, wheat, oats, and combines. Canasta, dominoes, deer hunting, and trotline fishing. Bob Wills, Ernest Tubb, Tommy Dorsey, and Glenn Miller. High school football, basketball, double-dating, Saturday afternoon movies, dances at a friend's house, and parking on a country lane.

I was hardly an informed, worldly citizen. To my knowledge, I never knew a Jew or a Catholic until I went to college. Well, in

Brady, the Rosenberg's had a clothing store, but I did not know them personally. Some of the itinerant Mexicans who picked cotton during season were probably Catholic, but it held no interest for me at the time. Lohn High was lily-white and most of us were pretty much unaware of what existed beyond the McCulloch County line.

Texas A&M from 1948 to 1952 was not a whole lot different in racial and sociological makeup than tiny Lohn, Texas. There were lots of students there from Dallas Houston, San Antonio and other Texas cities, but there were no blacks, no women and few Hispanics. Attitudes, experiences and beliefs were not all that varied. I did become close friends with Ted Walton, a Catholic and Dave Wolfe, a Jewish classmate.

My thoughts on race, gender and religion were pretty much what my grown-up influences taught me. I remember late night bull-sessions in the dorm where we argued whether there would ever be a black student at Texas A&M. Most of my classmates thought not. And, echoing their elders, they made it clear that they would never room with one, if blacks were ever admitted. I was liberal even then, or I thought I was, because I always argued that it wouldn't bother me to room with a black student.

My 27 years experience in the army was more enlightening and liberating as I worked with soldiers, NCO's and officers of almost every race, religion and ethnic origin.

So, my natural bent toward liberalism and my military experience wiped away all my ingrained prejudices and the last wisps of bigotry learned from childhood—I thought.

A few years ago, I had an emergency medical procedure in Austin. On the front door of the clinic, there was a list of names of the doctors who practiced there. Five of those names were of the common Anglo-Saxon variety, while the sixth name was obviously of an ethnicity other than my own.

The doctor did a magnificent job repairing my torn and detached retina; he had great compassion; and he was professional in every way.

On the way home, I confessed to my wife that I had some initial trepidation about the doctor who performed the procedure. I had a clear and conscious awareness of experiencing the prejudices that lingered from my youth. I felt guilty, self-conscious, and thoroughly chastened.

That is why I support Barack Obama. His inspirational oratory, his calm demeanor in dealing with the accusations and innuendos thrown at him; his remarkable achievements to this point; and his ability to articulate a vision for this country have caused me to begin looking deeper into my prejudices and examining them in a new light. That is what he has done for me.

What I believe Obama, as president of the United States, will do for me is change forever the dialogue in this country about race. I believe he can move us much closer to Martin Luther King's dream than we have ever been. I believe he can move us to a time when we will look beyond race, gender, or religion to judge character. bibb111231@ yahoo.com

I Been Thinkin'—Teens and the future

Often, I hear my peers and others, even younger than I—well, that includes almost everyone—belittling the teens of today. And in the interest of full disclosure, I too am guilty, at times, of putting down the younger generation. About the time, I think those under 30 have really gone to Hades in a hand-basket, I am confronted with something like the January 2, 2009 front page of the *S.A. Life* section of the *San Antonio Express-News*.

The article is titled "Dear Mr. President ..." and contains short messages from the 15 teens who comprise the San Antonio Express-News Teen Team. The team is asked to tell President-elect Obama of their hopes, concerns, expectations, and dreams.

As a reader of the op-ed pages of various newspapers, I peruse the thoughts of many erudite pundits who offer tons of advice to our elected officials. From what I see in the article cited above, I think our popular publications could benefit immensely by dipping into this pool of teen wisdom from time to time.

Individuals of the team address abortion, health care, college costs, driving age, immigration, Iraq, education, economy, climate change and a myriad of smaller issues. I must admit that some of the suggestions show the naiveté of the young writers and some are of the "in your dreams" variety. But, in general the short pieces are well-written, thought-provoking essays that reveal a knowledge and concern we rarely attribute to those not yet out of college, much less high school.

One teen, Madeleine McCaleb, chastises Obama for his stance on the abortion issue and pleads that he reconsider and be open to a more balanced perspective regarding that sensitive issue. Joy Freemyer suggests that the answer to the economic mess is not bailouts and handouts, but a more educated and responsible population. Caterina Gutierrez points out that immigrants, legal and illegal, make a huge contribution to the intellectual, educational, and social resources of the country as she urges Obama to help immigrants achieve their dream of becoming Americans.

All 15 of the essays are in this vein. But one caught my eye, largely because of its heading. Melissa Martin, a senior at Clark High School, titled her essay, "Remember…"

She begins by acknowledging that she lacks the wisdom to advise the President-to-be on policy matters. So, she has compiled a "simple list of reminders."

Her first reminder is the Republicans. She explains that while they may have made some bad decisions, half the people in the country voted for their policies, so reach across the aisle. Second, she urges Obama to remember the Rolling Stones. "You can't always get what you want," but if you really try, you will often get what you need.

Melissa then exhorts the President-elect to remember Abraham Lincoln when she quotes: "What is popular is not always right. What is right is not always popular." She goes on to point out that too often politicians try to please everyone all the time. Can't be done. She then, asks Obama to remember an unlikely character, Ferris Bueller, as she asserts that the young are smarter and certainly more clever than credited. She invokes Malia and Sasha at this point and asks that he attempt to give every American child the opportunity to excel that his daughters will receive.

The Dark Knight is her next reminder as she quotes the Michael Caine character, "Some men aren't looking for anything logical like money. …..Some men just want to watch the world burn." She goes on to say that, "It's vital to recognize when conflict is futile. It is just as important to recognize when it is not."

Last, she recommends Obama remember Ernest Hemingway. "Never confuse movement with action," she quotes. She ends her short list of admonitions with the admission that it might be quixotic, but maybe that's what teen-agers are about—seeing what's wrong with the world and trying to fix it.

In reality, all the essays are somewhat quixotic. But each one shows that young people are engaged. They are thinking. They are caring. Their concerns are deeper than prom dresses, varsity teams, Ipods, and cell phones. To me, it shows that beneath that façade of "teen cool" they present to us a depth of knowledge and understanding that will be honed by education, experience, failures, and successes. And they will produce a better world than we know today.

Obama/Warren

Why the huge dust-up about Obama's selection of Rick Warren to give the invocation at the inauguration? The op-ed pages of almost every paper have opinion pieces that come down on one side or the other. To me, an avowed liberal and an Obama supporter since 2004, his selection of Warren to give a two-minute prayer further proves Obama's intellectual fearlessness and his ability to respect a difference of opinion.

We liberals like to promote the notion of choice when discussing what we call a moral decision. Well, here's another liberal—Obama— who has exercised his freedom of choice and selected a right-leaning evangelical to participate in his inauguration. Within a week, the effect of that, in my view, will not be even a blip on the moral or political radar. However, media space is used by both sides to rant about it.

Katha Pollitt, an esteemed columnist for *The Nation*, writes in the *Austin American-Statesman* (12-30-08) that many Democrats are incensed over Obama's selection of Warren for the symbolically important task of delivering the inaugural invocation. She doesn't back that up with any research as she goes on to compare it, metaphorically, with McCain having Al Sharpton deliver the invocation at his imagined inaugural.

Warren, as most readers know, is the pastor of Saddleback Church in Orange County, California. He is also the author of *The Purpose Driven Life* and other books. Ms. Pollitt points out a list of Warren's anti-liberal sins: 1) led the fight in California to pass proposition 8, banning gay marriage; 2) espouses poisonous rhetoric against pro-choice proponents; 3) condemns all Jews—along with another two or three billion people—to hell for not believing in Christ; 4) is anti-evolutionist; 5) believes wives should be submissive to their husbands.

Ms. Pollitt castigates Obama for disrespecting those who worked so hard to get him elected. She writes: "I'm all for building bridges, but honoring Warren, who insults Obama's base as perverts and murderers, is definitely a bridge too far."

I see it a little differently. Rick Warren's belief is his business and the constitution of the United States guarantees that. However, when Rick Warren prays, I'm thinking he prays to the same God I do. I'm thinking that in his prayer, he will ask for that God's blessings on this country, and its people. That will include those who believe a woman has a right to determine what happens to her body; it will include those who love and cherish a person of the same sex; it will include all races and ethnicities; it will even include those who profess other religious beliefs.

Mr. Warren may have some off-the-wall—to us liberals—beliefs But it is my observation, based on my limited study of history, that arguments involving moral issues are won, not by reasoning, logic, or brilliant oratory of the protagonist. Rather, the arguments are lost by the eventual realization by mankind of the emptiness, cruelty, and wrong-headedness inherent in the belief, i.e., the right of one man to own another.

I see this as CHANGE WE CAN BELIEVE IN. It is a major departure from the last eight years where pandering has been the order of the day. Let's not forget Obama's words in 2004, when he so eloquently illustrated his vision for America:

"The pundits like to slice-and-dice our country into Red States and Blue States; Red States for Republicans, Blue States for Democrats. But I've got news for them too. We worship an "awesome God" in the Blue States and we don't like federal agents poking around in our libraries in the Red States. We coach Little League in the Blue States and, yes, we've got some gay friends in the Red States. There are patriots who opposed the war in Iraq and there are patriots who supported the war in Iraq. We are one people, all of us pledging allegiance to the stars and stripes, all of us defending the United States of America."

On the same page of the *Austin American-Statesman,* Kathryn Jean Lopez begins her column praising Obama's selection of Warren for the invocation at the inauguration. She goes on to say that, "… religious folks have been feeling marginalized from politics of late; Obama's choice caps off an election season that hit churchgoers hard."

As a fairly religious person and a churchgoer, I haven't a clue what Ms. Lopez is talking about. I haven't felt a bit marginalized from politics of late. I can only assume she thinks all Christians and churchgoers believe as she does.

She goes on to criticize those who have exercised their constitutional right to assemble and protest the passage of Proposition 8. She uses inflammatory terms such as "angry" and "vociferous" to describe the protestors and says that churches have been threatened. But, like Ms. Pollitt, Ms. Lopez makes claims with no evidence to support her assertions.

Strangely enough, she departs from her original premise and spends the rest of her column criticizing and deconstructing a recent *Newsweek* article that takes exception to the notion that the Bible explicitly prohibits gay marriage.

I guess I'm guilty of believing words mean what they have meant over the years; that "choice" means the right to choose; that "reaching out" means respecting the rights and beliefs of others; that "uniting" means coming together in harmony.

Political Signs

One of the things that has caught my attention is all the political signs around the countryside. The candidates put up signs throughout the county. I guess some put them in more than one county. They are at road intersections, in residential yards, in vacant lots, in the beds of pickups–that's one of the few times one will see anything besides a dog in the bed of a pickup.

I wonder if these signs serve any constructive purpose. Do people vote for a candidate based on how many signs they see scattered around the countryside? As I ask that question, I cringe to think that may be true. We do know that name recognition is a factor in people's voting, especially in cases involving positions where the elected official immediately becomes anonymous. Examples are appeal court judges or the State Board of Education or a candidate for the railroad commission. Not to say these offices aren't important. It is simply a fact that no one knows who occupies them after an election.

My disclaimer. When I go into the voting booth and see candidates for offices such as those mentioned above, I tend to vote for the name I recognize, even if the recognition is vague and beyond relating to anything significant. I admit to an occasional perverse reaction to too much name recognition and vote against an obnoxious candidate. See following paragraph.

Name recognition matters and the most egregious case of one taking advantage of a familiar name was the ubiquitous Gene Kelly. He was a retired Air Force colonel and lawyer who ran for statewide office in Texas six times. He ran for the Texas Supreme Court, the Court of Criminal Appeals, attorney general, and the U.S. Senate. He once came in a close second in a race for a seat on the Supreme Court.

For those of you under 30, who might accidentally find yourself reading this newspaper, Gene Kelly was also the name of a famous movie actor, singer and dancer. His most famous movie, to my recollection, was *April in Paris* and his most famous song and scene was *Singing in the Rain*, in that movie.

OK, name recognition matters. So, what does it cost to have your name plastered all over the county? I have no idea. I can only surmise that the local sign makers greet every election with glee. The more candidates, the more signs. It occurs to me that sign makers should solicit someone to run against an unopposed candidate, if only to stimulate the economy.

Are there any rules and regulations governing signs? How big can they be? How much money can a candidate spend on campaign publicity? That opens a whole new area of inquiry if we go to statewide offices where TV is a major player. For the purpose of this piece, I'm limiting my interest to local elections. I consider state representative a local election.

Are local elections affected by the recent Supreme Court ruling that corporations can spend an unlimited amount of money in support of a given candidate? Can we have a Wal-Mart city council? Is it possible Kyle could have a Mayor Cabela. Certainly that name has recognition.

I have often wondered what the defeated candidate does with his/her signs. I know what some do with them. They leave them to clutter the landscape for the next several months.

Speaking of cluttering the landscape, those out there now are pretty gross. That doesn't mean they aren't effective. In advertising, it is often said that the more irritating the ad, the more attention it gets and the more lasting its impression on the brain.

I googled "headache remedy ads," and HeadOn—remember the irritating commercial for this product—was the first one to come up. One commentator wrote: "The person in charge of HeadOn's advertising should be given a migraine and then forced to watch that commercial over and over while applying the product." He went on to explain the product does not work. But, how much of that stuff did they sell?

So, I'm guessing that about 90 percent of political advertising has little or no relation to actual facts, truth, or integrity. The nice thing about signs is that a candidate can't make many claims. About all he/she can put on a sign are words such as: Experienced, Honest, Conservative, For All the People. One candidate this election has used the word, Wanted in bold letters. It gets your attention. But most candidates know what we do when we go to the voting booth. We look for names we recognize. Ergo, their names are huge on the signs. That is what we are supposed to see. The office for which the candidate is running is barely visible on most of the signs.

In spite of the importance of name recognition, I can proudly say I have never voted for Gene Kelly for anything.

President's Race—2008

We have been bombarded for about a year with wall to wall coverage of the presidential primaries on TV and in newspapers. It all began with about eight Democrats and nine Republicans vying for the nomination. Some of those, I'm sure, never thought for a minute that they had a chance to win, but it was a great platform from which to trumpet their particular cause. Some were Johnny One-note candidates, i.e., Tom Tancredo whose only issue seemed to be immigration. Illegal immigration.

The pundits have written that our system for selecting candidates, or presidents for that matter, is arcane, inefficient, and ridiculous. Some have written that the old smoke-filled rooms at the conventions, where deals were made and principles were sacrificed in the pursuit of power were better than the primary system of today.

It is about here that I should issue my disclaimer. I am not a historian. What follows is based on my memory, the conventional wisdom at the time, or is gleaned from my cursory readings of history. So, I'm not passing judgment on our political process. I'm sharing with you some thoughts to consider.

There has been much talk among the candidates and in the debates about who is best qualified to be president. Some say "this experience better qualifies me to lead the nation." Others say "that experience better qualifies me to lead the nation." On the matter of qualifications, no matter who might be the candidate, I think we are, as Aunt Molly used to say, "gettin' a pig in a poke." My thought is that our first four or five presidents were virtually anointed and fell into the office almost as a rite of passage. They were aristocrats who were instrumental in the Revolution and in the formation of the governments that followed.

They were intellectuals with formidable resumes in responsible positions. They had their differences. For instance, Jefferson thought he should have been the second president. Instead he became the vice-president, whereupon, he left Washington and went home to Virginia for 11 months.

This campaign will wear on for another 10 months and we will hear a flood of political rhetoric, incessant reporting of the latest gaffe by this or that candidate, and breathless analysis of the ubiquitous polls. What will we learn about these people that will help us select the most qualified person to lead the nation?

My answer. Nothing.

We may learn about their dog, Checkers (Nixon); or that they voted against it before they voted for it (Kerry); or that they were brainwashed (*George* Romney); or some other nonsensical bit of personal history which has absolutely no bearing on what kind of president they would be.

Looking at some of the qualifications of past presidents, I think Aunt Molly was absolutely right. We're getting a "pig in a poke," no matter who is eventually elected.

Lincoln was nominated in 1860 through some wily maneuvering to get the Republican convention held in Chicago. He was a man with almost no formal education; he had served in the state legislature; he had lost in his bid to become a senator. He was opposed by three rather distinguished individuals. Seward had served as governor of New York and senator from that state. Chase had also served as governor of Ohio, had a national reputation and a strong following among the anti-slavery crowd. Bates had a distinguished political career in Missouri and was popular in the west.

Franklin Roosevelt was initially considered to be a fop and an intellectual lightweight. For the first 12 years of my life I thought "president" and Roosevelt were one word. He has been rated by historians among the top five greatest presidents of all time.

Harry Truman, like Lincoln, had little formal education. He was considered a hick farmer, failed haberdasher, and tool of the Kansas City Pendergast machine. In 1948, it was a forgone conclusion that Thomas Dewey would defeat him in a landslide. Truman is credited with keeping the Russian expansion in check and successfully conducting the Cold War without allowing it to become a wider hot war, Korea aside. His stock has risen significantly since he left office.

It has been said that no one was more ready to be president than Lyndon Johnson. His congressional experience, his knowledge of politics and his awareness of world affairs made him a natural to lead the nation. His conduct of the Viet Nam war resulted in his refusal to run for a second term.

Richard Nixon had served admirably in congress. He had been at the seat of power as vice-president for eight years. His experience, like that of Lyndon, was thought to make him ideally qualified for the job. We all know how that turned out.

So, as the primaries whittle the list of candidates, it becomes a matter of who can survive for the next 10 months. And, history tells us that no matter who the ultimate survivor might be, we're going to "get a pig in a poke."

Religion & Politics

For those of you who believe that a religious litmus test is essential for a presidential candidate, you can stop reading now.

Congress shall make no law respecting an establishment of religion or prohibiting the free exercise thereof... (From the First Amendment, the U.S. Constitution)

In my view, all this hubbub about the religious beliefs of presidential candidates is probably the greatest waste of time since the introduction of the Edsel automobile.

Recently, Mr. Romney felt the need to go on television and, in the footsteps of John F. Kennedy, explain his relationship to the Mormon Church and how that would affect his ability to abide by the constitution. It would not, he said.

That got me thinkin'. What were the religious views of past presidents? Being research-challenged, I googled (that's now a verb, I understand) a few and found remarkable information about some of our more prominent leaders of the past.

Since this column is space-limited, references are omitted. All the comments regarding the presidents can be found by googling (verb) their name and "religious views."

Under Washington there is a story of Lord Beaconsfield who was asked what religion he followed. Beaconsfield replied, "The religion of wise men." Pushing further, the questioner asked what religion is that. "Wise men never tell," the Lord answered. Washington is then described as a wise man.

I have read in more than one publication that Washington, after taking the oath of the presidency, ad libbed the "So help me God" part. Of course, it has remained a part of the oath ever since. But, was that a Christian God, to whom he referred?

It is established beyond doubt that he did not take communion. He did not kneel in prayer, and it is doubtful anyone ever saw him pray. Upon Washington's departure from the presidency, he was visited by a group of ministers to discuss his religious views. Their goal was to elicit a sentiment with which to counter the infidelity of Thomas Paine. "The result was that orthodoxy received no more comfort than heterodoxy." The writer further asserts that evidence points strongly to Washington's being a Deist.

At his death bed there were three doctors, but no ministers. It is said he died like an ancient pagan Greek or Roman.

John Adams, our second president, was raised a Congregationalist, but rejected many fundamental doctrines of Christianity, such as the Trinity and the divinity of Jesus. His father urged him to become a minister, but Adams was drawn to law, as he considered it to be a nobler calling.

David McCullough in *John Adams* points out that Adams became renowned as a lawyer when he successfully defended six *British* soldiers accused of killing innocent colonials in the Boston massacre. That would be the equivalent of John Edwards successfully defending a Muslim terrorist accused of murder. What do you think would happen to his poll numbers were this the case today?

Adams' view of religion was ambivalent. He believed it could be a force for good in individuals and for society at large, but his intellectual pursuits led him to believe that this was true for all religions, not just Christianity.

Thomas Jefferson was reluctant to discuss his religious beliefs. It is said that he was influenced by English deists and in the spirit of enlightenment, wrote his nephew, Peter Carr, in 1787, "Question with boldness even the existence of God; because if there be one, he must more approve the homage of reason, than that of blindfolded fear."

Jefferson was a leader in the effort to insure separation of church and state. Again, he wrote in the Statute of Virginia for Religious Freedom, "The legitimate powers of government extend to such acts as are injurious to others. But it does me no injury for my neighbor to say there are twenty gods or no god."

In the late 1790's Jefferson was accused of being an atheist. My guess is that arose from Alexander Hamilton who battled Jefferson during the bitter party conflict between the Federalists and the Republicans.

On June 25th, 1819, Jefferson wrote to Ezra Stiles, concerning his beliefs, "I am of a sect by myself, as far as I know."

It is said that, as a young man, Abraham Lincoln wrote a book on infidelity (non-belief, in this case) which was an attack on Christianity and the idea that Jesus was the Christ. When he ran for Congress against one Peter Cartwright in 1846, he was accused of being an infidel and an atheist. He never denied it. First, because it could and would be proved, and second, because he was too true to his own convictions to deny it.

A more thorough listing of why Lincoln rejected Christianity includes assertions that he did not believe in the Creation; he did not believe that the Bible was a special revelation from God; he did not believe in Christian miracles; he believed in universal inspiration and miracles under law; he did not believe in the divinity of Christ; he believed all things, matter and mind, were governed by laws, universal, absolute and eternal.

Lincoln was a realist, a very concrete thinker, and a pragmatist. From Doris Kerns Goodwin's book, *A Team of Rivals,* we learn that his position on slavery defies conventional wisdom. He did not campaign as an anti-slavery candidate. He campaigned as a candidate opposing the expansion of slavery. It was only when freeing the slaves became a practical matter and provided a military advantage to the North that he issued the Emancipation Proclamation.

I am not writing to argue religion. I merely wish to point out that to many of the great leaders—the founders and saviors of this nation—religion was irrelevant.

Have we become so narrow and bigoted in our thinking that we would bar a Jefferson, Lincoln, or Washington from the Presidency?

Vice Presidents

In a recent Democratic Party debate between Barack Obama and Hillary Clinton, the moderator asked: "Is there a chance there will be a Clinton/Obama or an Obama/Clinton ticket in the general election?" Of course, neither candidate answered the question.

But that got me thinkin' about vice presidents and their impact on the election. It is my theory that *no one* votes for the vice-president. And then I mused—aside from those who have succeeded to the presidency, and the current sitting veep, how many vice-presidents can you name? That's what I thought.

I can name only one, John Nance Garner. He was Franklin Roosevelt's first vice-president and he is famous for describing the job as, "Not worth a bucket of warm spit." I'm reasonably sure the quote was paraphrased by the press so that it could appear in a family newspaper.

Second place, as the New England Patriots will attest, is somewhere below the thrill of kissing your sister. The footprints of most vice-presidents have long since been washed away by the tide of events.

This is not to say that there have not been capable men in the job. This has been shown by the numerous vice-presidents who have succeeded to the presidency by one means or another.

Beginning with John Adams, who succeeded Washington, there have been many who left their mark on the nation and the world. Jefferson, Adams's vice-president, apparently had a disdain equal to Garner's for the job. In his day, the vice-president was the person who received the second highest vote total from the House of Representatives. When Jefferson, who vied with Adams for the presidency, found that he was the Vice-President, he promptly left Washington and spent the next 11 months at his home in Virginia.

Jefferson, then unseated Adams and his vice-president was Aaron Burr. Burr is probably best remembered as the man who killed Alexander Hamilton in a duel. As a result of that act, he is the only sitting vice-president to be indicted for murder. He fled south where he attempted to incite Louisiana to secede from the union and, with help from Spain, form an independent country.

Our vice-presidents have not been without a degree of notoriety. But, how many of you, dear readers, could identify the following names without a score card: George Clinton, Eldridge Gerry, Daniel Thompkins, Richard Johnson, George Dallas or William Rufus Devane King. They all served as vice-president for varied lengths of time between 1805 and 1853. William King served the third shortest time of any VP to date. He died in office after 45 days.

John Tyler, who succeeded William Henry Harrison, served the shortest time, only 31 days, before Harrison's death from pneumonia.

There have been14 vice-presidents who succeeded to the presidency. In spite of Garner's and Jefferson's disdain for the office, it is not a position without frightening potential or peril, depending on one's point of view.

After succeeding to the presidency, Thomas Jefferson expanded the nation's frontier with the Louisiana Purchase. Harry Truman made the choice to drop the atomic bomb; he was faced with the reconstruction of Europe and Japan; and he faced the communist world in the Cold War. Andrew Johnson took over shortly after Appomattox. Teddy Roosevelt established the national parks system. Lyndon Johnson presided over the nation's Viet Nam quagmire. Richard Nixon left the presidency in disgrace.

There have been attempts to strengthen the office of the Vice-President. As I understand it, the vice-president's only constitutionally mandated duty is to preside over the senate when he chooses to attend the deliberations.

Frequently, the vice-president has been chided by the press and late-night comedians over the frequency with which he is required to represent the president at funerals of foreign dignitaries.

Our current vice-president, Richard Bruce Cheney, has been described as the most powerful man to hold the office. A former member of the House and a seasoned bureaucrat who had occupied powerful posts in government before becoming VP, he was much more knowledgeable of the system in Washington than the President at the outset of the Bush administration. Consequently, he has been credited with responsibility for some of the major decisions of the current administration. Many suggest that the notion to invade Iraq came largely from the office of the Vice-President.

One of the things Mr. Cheney has done is muddy the water over the branch of government to which the office of the VP belongs. It was, at one time, thought to be a part of the executive branch, but as a result of a congressional inquiry, I understand Mr. Cheney declared it a part of the legislative branch, based on his duties to preside over the Senate.

At any rate, it is a somewhat nebulous position. Depending on the president, he may have lots or no power. Yet, the cliché is true: he or she is only a heartbeat away from the presidency.

So, should Garner and Jefferson rethink their attitude toward the office? And, will there be an Obama/Clinton or Clinton/Obama ticket?

I been thinkin'—not.

Gun Control

It has been four months, or thereabouts, since the Sandy Hook massacre. Fortunately, the issue of gun control has not dimmed like the memory of a bad dream. Those unfortunate families of New Town, Connecticut seem determined to keep it alive in the interest of the children and teachers who lost their lives in a senseless, almost unspeakable act of terror on December 14, 2012.

If we set aside the fact that the National Rifle Association (NRA) is an extremely powerful lobbying group for the arms industry, can there be any *real* purpose in resisting reasonable measures that would limit assault rifles, 30 round magazines, and background checks?

While I'm not an expert on hunting, it is a fact that I grew up with one of the all time champion deer hunters of his day. My Uncle Bill was an expert marksman and an avid hunter. He got his buck every year. In fact, he often got his friends' bucks every year. During the fall, venison was a staple at our table.

My memory tells me Uncle Bill owned two deer rifles over the time I knew him. The first one was a .30 Remington. It was a pump action weapon that held about six rounds. It required the shooter to pull the sleeve, located under the barrel, to eject the spent cartridge and chamber the new round. An expert such as Uncle Bill could probably fire six rounds accurately in about a minute. One did not have the option of pressing the trigger and spraying bullets over an area the size of a theater or a classroom.

His second deer rifle was a .300 Savage. He was a man of few emotions, but when he purchased that particular weapon, he was ecstatic. It was a semi-automatic. He only had to pull the trigger for every round fired. However, he did not have to disturb his aim by emptying the chamber with a pumping action. It held five rounds. As a deer hunter, he seldom had to use more than one round.

When I arrived in Viet Nam in 1965, troops were armed with the M-14 rifle. It was alleged to be an improvement over the WWII M-1. Perhaps it was, but just barely. Those whose age and memory parallel my own, will recall that the M-1 clip (not magazine) held eight rounds. The M-14 had a similar capability. It should be pointed out that the U.S. Army infantry soldier went through WWII rather successfully armed with a rifle that could be loaded with nine rounds, i.e., one in the chamber and eight in the clip.

Not long after my arrival in Viet Nam, I was fortunate enough to be assigned to an infantry battalion. Shortly after joining the battalion, the M-14 was replaced with the AR-15, a version of the now-infamous M-16. It had a variable capacity magazine and fired a .223 caliber round which was smaller than the .30 caliber of the M-14. That made for a lighter load for the infantryman who carried his ammo supply on his person.

The lighter weight and the rapid fire capability of the AR-15 were supposed to improve the capability of the U.S. infantryman. However, the rifle tended to jam when fired fully automatic. It was also more sensitive to maintenance and weather conditions than the M-1 or the M-14.

Early on, the Viet Cong (VC) were generally armed with rather primitive rifles provided by or abandoned by the French. Later, the North Viet Nam Army (NVA) was armed with the AK-47. American troops recognized the superiority of the AK-47 over the AR-15 and lack of compatible ammunition is the only thing that kept U.S. troops from using captured AK-47s.

Actually, the most popular weapon among infantrymen in Viet Nam was the shotgun. We were issued a few 12 gauge shotguns with a five round capacity. The point man was given the privilege of carrying the shotgun because he was most likely to encounter the enemy first, up close and personal. The shotgun was popular because one round usually dispatched the target and in the dense jungle growth, the shooter did not have to be an expert marksman.

So, what's the point of this lengthy preamble? First, if you can't kill a deer, an elk, a moose, or any other defenseless animal with five rounds you should not be hunting. Second, if you want to own a weapon for self-protection, get a shotgun. Almost anyone can be an effective shooter with a shotgun against an intruder or a predator. Very little training required. Point, pull and protect.

So, give me a good argument for owning an AK-47, or an M-16 or a 30 round magazine. Please.

Second Amendment? First Amendment says, "Congress shall make no law…abridging the freedom of speech, or the press…." However, we all agree that one is not free to shout "fire" in a crowded theater when there is no reason to shout "fire." Nor is the press free to publish libel. So, why can't we control the sale of weapons whose only purpose is to kill people—in bunches?

As to the matter of background checks, doesn't it make sense to verify the mental health or the criminal history of a gun owner? As a mental health professional for 20 years or so, I am very much aware that there are the unfortunate among us who suffer hallucinations and other distortions in their thought processes that result in tragedies such as Littleton, Aurora and Sandy Hook. Not to say those perpetrators were mentally ill. I do not know this. But, surely it would serve the general good to be aware of a person's history before providing him/her with a weapon of mass destruction.

Lincoln, the Movie

The screen introduction to the movie, *Lincoln,* announces that it is based in part on the Doris Kearns Goodwin book, *Team of Rivals.* Indeed, it is based on a very small part of that book. Nevertheless, it is a dramatic depiction of Lincoln's determination to pass the 13th Amendment to the Constitution. It also dramatizes Lincoln's difficult moral choice between insuring the elimination of slavery in America and possibly ending the war months earlier, thereby saving thousands of lives.

One of my immediate reactions to the film was that Lyndon Baines Johnson was not the first, arm-twister in American politics who believed that the end justified the means. While Lincoln is revered today as the savior of the Union and the Great Emancipator, this movie illustrates with believable drama the lengths to which he was willing to go to get the 13th Amendment passed.

The film is replete with implications of financial bribery, promises of plum offices in home states, and other dubious means of insuring passage of the amendment by the House of Representatives. Goodwin notes this in passing in her book, but Spielberg highlights it in the film and it makes for high drama.

The parallel story in this film is Lincoln's private life in the White House. Mary Todd Lincoln is shown to be the complex, see-saw character that history has confirmed. At times Lincoln's family life was tranquil and pleasant. At other times, Mary was demanding and somewhat paranoid. According to Goodwin, she never recovered from the death of her favorite child, Willie, who died in the White House. A tense scene between her and Lincoln reveals his concern over her sanity, following Willie's death.

As was his practice in governing, Lincoln managed a cool exterior in family matters, no matter the depth of feeling. He is shown on more than one occasion deflecting difficult and painful situations, both personal and political, with anecdotes gleaned from his early days as a circuit-riding lawyer or a poor man making his way on the western frontier.

Daniel Day-Lewis turns in an Oscar-worthy performance as Lincoln. He captures the humble, yet steadfast character that was the private Lincoln. Further, he makes believable the dedication along with the brilliance and perseverance that was the political Lincoln, especially as Commander-in-Chief.

Sally Fields, as Mary Todd Lincoln, turns in a commendable performance that should resurrect her career. I think she will, once again, realize that Hollywood, "really, really likes [her]," though she may not get an Oscar.

Tommy Lee Jones, playing Thaddeus Stevens, the sarcastic, abrasive radical Republican member of the House of Representatives, gives us another acting highlight. Well, he actually just plays Tommy Lee Jones, but, for me, that's always an acting highlight. Radical, rigid, unyielding, curmudgeon that he is, the Stevens character illustrates in a gripping scene that, even for him, the end justifies the means as he denies his own well-known, long-held beliefs in order to influence the critical vote for the 13th Amendment.

I should also mention David Strathairn's performance as William Seward, Lincoln's Secretary of State. He was probably Lincoln's most feared rival for the presidency, but, in the film, he is shown to be the president's staunchest ally, supporting and encouraging him at the most difficult and darkest of times. As Seward did for Lincoln, Straithairn's performance provides an essential continuity to the film.

As one walks out of the movie and reflects on the political landscape of today, one can't help noting "......the more things change, the more they remain the same."

Go to the movie. Get an entertaining lesson in how government really works and remember the torturous path this country has trod to get where we are today.

Steroids and Baseball

The latest cable news round-the-clock, 24/7, talking-head topic is the baseball steroid scandal. Admittedly, it is more palatable than Brittany, Lindsey or Paris, but is it really significant?

Well, yes.

In 1957 and 1958, I watched a slender, soft-spoken, unassuming kid from Alabama who wore jersey number 44 and played right-field for the Milwaukee Braves. Compared to teammates Eddie Mathews and Joe Adcock, he was an unimposing figure on the baseball field. But he could run, he could throw and he had the quickest wrists in baseball. He hung around the league after most of his teammates were finished. When he did retire he had hit 755 home runs.

Hank Aaron's record of 755 homers was denigrated because "the ball was livelier," "the parks were smaller," "pitchers were not as good as those of Ruth's era." Further, he was besmirched and—yes, hated—for breaking the most hallowed record in baseball. But, he was never accused of using drugs, especially performance enhancing drugs. He did put on a few pounds in his later years, but those were age-induced and he would, no doubt, tell you they were more of a hindrance than a help.

Warren Spahn and Lew Burdette would pitch the Braves to two National League pennants and one World Series Championship during that time.

They were icons—Spahn's 363 wins is the most by any left-hander in baseball—and heroes and rightfully so. Every kid in America, regardless of age, imagined himself an Aaron, a Spahn, or a Burdette.

While baseball still bills itself as America's pastime, it is probably second in popularity to football—college and pro. Nevertheless, it remains an integral part of the fabric of American life. Kids still collect baseball cards; kids are still thrilled with their first fielder's glove; and kids still have visions of hitting the game winning home run of the World Series. Attendance records are broken each year and the minor leagues are enjoying resurgence. Baseball and the people who play it are still relevant in the United States, not to mention South America and Japan.

So, why do I care if some over-paid athlete pumps himself up with steroids to enhance his statistics and improve his bargaining power when contract-signing time rolls around? Why do I care if he is risking high blood pressure, heart disease, blood clots, stroke, liver damage, liver cancer, ligament and tendon damage, impotence, and enlarged prostate?

I care because Cameron, my 14 year-old grandson is an excellent athlete and an outstanding student. I care because he plays baseball in highly competitive leagues. I care because he plays high school basketball. I care because at five feet, seven inches tall and 120 pounds, he is not as big and as strong as many of his contemporaries. He compensates for his lack of size and strength with speed, coordination and understanding of the game.

He is playing for highly competitive coaches who want to win. He is playing with kids whose parents have spent lots of money on camps and special tutoring to insure their kids make the team and get noticed by coaches at the next level.

When I see the pressure on these kids today, I wonder what limits will be tested in the pursuit of athletic dominance. If major league baseball players—the Clemens, Pettittes, Palmeiras, Tejedas, McGuires, Bonds, Sheffields and some 78 other major leaguers are using, it would seem an easy argument to convince a young impressionable kid that, it is the thing to do.

Many of these parents and the kids have visions of college scholarships and professional contracts in their future. So, what does it take to get there? How tempting is it for a coach—or a parent—to convince a kid he needs to "bulk up" to get to the next level? The old saw, "They all do it," would not only be plausible, it would be truthful.

119

A year or so ago People magazine ran an article about a young high school football player in Plano, Texas who committed suicide as a result of steroid use. My guess is that he was just one of thousands and his case received nation-wide publicity because the outcome was the most dramatic and tragic.

I hope Major League Baseball will work diligently to reclaim the legacy established by the Aarons, Spahns, Ruths, Mantles, and Williamses (Ted). I hope Major League Baseball will clean up its act so that Cameron can dream of hitting that game-winning home run in the World Series without thinking he has to have chemical enhancement to do it.

I Been Thinkin'—Bowl Games

Back when there were only about 27 football bowl games at the end of the season, I wrote a column on the proliferation of bowl games and the ridiculousness of it all. Of course, I don't suppose it is so ridiculous when one considers that it's all about the money. But even so, there ought to be a limit.

OK, this year there are 35 bowl games. And that's where the ridiculous part starts, but does not necessarily end. They started on December 15 and will not end until January 7th of 2013. That's about three weeks of bowl games. As I recall, the argument the NCAA has always used for not having a playoff system to determine the national champion has been that it would require players to be away from the classroom for too long. This bowl schedule makes a travesty of that argument and maybe that is what has moved the NCAA to make a first move toward a playoff in the near future.

The names of some of the bowls define ridiculous. Here are a few examples: *The Beef O'Brady Bowl*, really; the *Little Caesars Bowl*, come on; *Heart o' Dallas Bowl*, are you kidding; *Buffalo Wild Wings Bowl*, enough awready; but the worst name for a bowl game...*The Idaho Potato Bowl*, give me a break. That bowl beat out the *Pinstripe Bowl*.

So, I'm old. I live in a world of nostalgia and I recognize it. But it seems there should be a limit to what we will expose ourselves. OK, I know, it's all about the money. According to Google, there are 119 NCAA teams in the Football Bowl Subdivision, meaning that almost 60 percent of the teams are going to a bowl.

Back in the day—50s and 60s—there were six or seven bowls all held on or about New Years Day. *The Rose Bowl* was the granddaddy of them all. Then there were the *Orange Bowl*, the *Cotton Bowl* and the *Sugar Bowl*. (An aside here: El Paso's *Sun Bowl* is actually older than the *Cotton Bowl*, but

121

never reached the same level of prestige.) These bowls were the heavy-hitters, but they were supported by some pretty decent bowls, such as the *Gator Bowl,* the aforementioned *Sun Bowl,* the *Peach Bowl* and the *Independence Bowl.* I probably missed one or two, but I do have limited space.

Teams that played in those bowls were worthy teams with records that made some sense. The Big Ten champion played the Pac 10 champion in the *Rose Bowl;* The Southwest Conference Champion played some worthy opponent, frequently from the Southeastern Conference in the *Cotton Bowl. The Orange Bowl* and the *Sugar Bowl* hosted nationally prominent teams, usually featuring some outstanding players.

Who is going to attend these bowl games? Well, the alums who have become big donors to the respective school's athletic programs are going. They will get to rub shoulders with the coaches and players, as well as receive special treatment by the bowl sponsor. I suppose the CEOs of the sponsoring corporation and their guests will attend. Local press and beat reporters will have a place in the press box.

How many SMU students will go to the *Sheraton Hawaii Bowl,* played in Honolulu on Christmas Eve? And do you suppose a large number of USC students will travel to El Paso to see the *Sun Bowl* game between USC and Georgia Tech? I admit there will be a sizable student representation from Texas A&M at the Cotton Bowl. Perhaps a large portion of the Corps and the band will be on hand. No doubt, Vanderbilt student body will be well represented as their team takes on North Carolina State in the *Music City Bowl,* as it will be played in Nashville, home of Vandy.

Actually, there are some very attractive locations for these games. Las Vegas, San Diego, Orlando and New Orleans are a few of the more esoteric locations. However, games are played in Shreveport, Fort Worth, Houston, and Detroit. Who is going to travel there to see the *Independence Bowl,* the *Armed Forces Bowl, Meineke Car Care Bowl* and the *Little Caesar's Pizza Bowl?*

One internet listing of the bowl games does not even list the location, just the TV network and the date and time. One can conclude that college football, as well as the pros (is there a difference?) has been captured by TV and its insatiable commercial appetite. Who benefits from all this proliferation? I guess the end result which is money benefits a large number of people and institutions, but the players benefit least of all.

Women Football Analysts/Reporters

It is now the middle of the football season and it is time someone spoke up about a travesty that has been foisted on every football fan who thinks the game should retain a modicum of credibility. I recognize that I am inviting a firestorm of criticism akin to that created when John Kerry inadvertently put his foot in his mouth. The difference is I'm not trying to make a joke.

I have watched the game change over time. I won't even go into describing my high school football experience, except to say, it was so long ago we really did use leather helmets; the jerseys had small numbers; we still had "ends" as opposed to "wideouts." There were halfbacks and fullbacks, as opposed to running backs and the quarterback decided which play to run. Substitution was limited. OK, so there have been changes that improved the game.

Television changed the game even more. My first experience with football broadcasting was listening to Kern Tipps, Lindsey Nelson and Curt Gowdy on the radio. They did a great job of painting a word picture of the game. They could create excitement and color which was more enthralling than the game action.

Then came television. Black and white. One of the most memorable sports experiences of my life was watching the 1958 National Football League championship game between the New York Giants and the Baltimore Colts. Yes, Virginia, there was a great football team called the *Baltimore* Colts until a greedy owner snaked them out of town under the cover of darkness. It was the first professional game decided in overtime and the Colts managed to defeat the Giants 23-17 on an Alan Ameche one-yard plunge.

Chris Schenkel called the play by play and Chuck Thompson did the color. There were no amateur announcers on the sidelines to interfere with the flow of the game and the erudite description and analysis provided by the professionals in the booth. And certainly there were no *female* announcers along the sidelines.

Somewhere, somehow, at some time, somebody decided we needed to hear the minutia of sideline activity and all the clichés of coach-speak, during the game. So, they started out with the Lynn Swanns, the Armen Katayians, and Erik Dickersons. While I think they added little to the game, they, at least, had credibility. They had either played the game or had a credible sports announcer's vitae. Most of the time, I could understand what they were saying and they provided a bit of added insight into the game.

Then, someone decided all sideline announcers had to be female. Well, Tony Siragusa, a real football player, survives in this gender-equality charade.

I can never understand what these female announcers are saying. To be honest, I don't listen very closely. They begin telling us that Jamal has a broken shoe string and must come out of the game for one play about the time the time 83,000 people start screaming. Even worse, they face the camera and emote as if they were announcing the start of World War III, as they report that Coach Cower said he would stay with Big Ben in the second half, despite two interceptions and a fumble which led to 21 points for the opposition.

I have to wonder if they know Ben Roethlisberger from the couturier who selects their faux fur fashions.

Suzy Kolber, Michelle Tafoya, Lisa Guerrero, Leslie Visser, Bonnie Bernstein, and Pam Oliver are all, no doubt, brilliant and have paid their dues in broadcasting. And while I'm being chauvinistic, I suppose I should add that they are all reasonably attractive. They may very well know Big Ben from the guy who selects their hats and coats, but they lack CREDIBILITY.

Football is a guy thing. If each of those women was more articulate than Michaels; could out-BAM!! Madden; and could dissect the game better than Troy; it still wouldn't work for me.

I want to add a disclaimer here. I could probably be labeled a feminist, based on my general attitude toward women. I am thrilled to see Danica

Patrick in the Indy 500, Carly Fiorini as CEO of Hewlett-Packard; and Julie Krone, first female jockey inducted into the Racing Hall of Fame.

But, I must say my wife, who grew up in Steeler country, agrees with me about women sideline announcers at football games. Somehow, it is like putting on a striped tie with a checked shirt. They just don't match. Now, a 300 pound Tony Siragusa, competing with Bill Belicek for "most likely to be nabbed by the fashion police," explaining the most mundane aspect of the game in two syllable words—that works—it's credible.

Working Out

The gym—I go to the Student Recreation Center (SRC) at Texas State—was sparsely populated this Friday morning, Only the die-hards were there, and not all of them. As I noted the lack of participants, I asked my self why I do this. Why didn't I stay in bed, this morning, catch a few more Zees and wait for the sun to awaken me?

At 5:45 this morning I was snugly ensconced in my bed, in a state of semi-consciousness, contemplating the pleasure that would ensue if I pulled the covers over my head and went back to sleep. However, that little irritant called a conscience began whispering all sorts of admonitions such as "lazy," "sloppy," "consistent," and "regret." So, against every common sense thought I could muster, I tossed back the covers and forced my feet to the floor.

Following my bathroom ablutions, I made it to the kitchen and prepared a pot of fresh coffee. A cup of coffee and perusal of the Austin American-Statesman sports pages and I drug my bike from under the house and headed to the gym. By this time, I was reasonably awake and semi-ready to work out.

Did you ever notice how much a modern gym, with all its exercise machines, resembles the old torture chambers depicted in books about the Spanish Inquisition? There is a definite resemblance. Today, we voluntarily subject ourselves to the torture of these machines.

In the last 30 years or so exercise gyms have gained a foothold among the general population. As a kid, living in a rural area, I saw no one exercise for the fun of it, or the results it produced. Oh, we got plenty of exercise. It was called work. There was cotton to be chopped, picked, weighed and ginned. There was corn to be pulled, and scooped into the barn. Hay bales, grain sacks, feed bundles and equipment had to be lifted, moved, stored and stacked by hand. Not everyone had a car. Walking more than a city block was not a rare occurrence. Frequently water had to be carried from the well to the house; clothes were hung on a line to dry.

We had athletic teams in school, but even in college, the teams only worked out during the season. It was not a year-round process.

So, having said all that, why do I go to the torture chamber three days a week for an hour or more and subject myself to pain, misery and exhaustion? As I asked that question this particular Friday morning, I listened to myself. And I got the answer.

That hour on Monday, Wednesday and Friday makes the other 165 hours of the week a lot more pleasant. I credit my quality of life with an almost uninterrupted pursuit of physical conditioning which began in 1967. It was then I discovered *Aerobics,* a book by Dr. Ken Cooper. That book is responsible for the running/jogging craze that still attracts a large number of participants. I ran for years until my knees gave out. That's when I got a bike. Thanks to my workouts, I enjoy an active life-style. A large part of our summers in Colorado consist of hiking, cycling and tennis.

When I go to the SRC, I am surrounded by flat bellies and round bottoms. When I hear people talking about the lack of energy, ambition, and initiative of young people, all I need do is glance around the gym. I'm surrounded by 18-22 year olds who are up at 5:00 AM, in the gym at 6:00 and in class by 8:00. They amaze me with their work ethic in the pursuit of self-improvement and conditioning. There is a generation out there that is better than the one before.

I have never been mistaken for a power-lifter or a body builder, but I admit, I love it when those young students ask my age and are awed when I tell them. I am a bit of a narcissist.

As I grow older, I know there are parts of me that are going to fail. I am told that there are people in the nursing homes simply because they don't have the strength to get out of bed. I toss those covers back each morning to test my ability to get out of bed. I'm also told more people die in the hospital than any other place. If I'm going to achieve my goal of living 100 years, I need to stay out of the hospital. And if I'm gong to enjoy it, I need to stay out of the nursing home.

But, I don't stop with the physical workouts. They tell me the brain, like the body, tends to deteriorate with time and that intellectual pursuits will forestall that deterioration. So, where is my crossword puzzle?

Golf

Golf is addictive. It replaces the drugs. It replaces the alcohol. I see it as a natural progression. I suppose that if you survive your drug, you have golf ahead of you.

Dennis Hopper in the April, 2001 issue of Maximum Golf.

Golf is not a game. It is not a sport. It is an addiction. No less an authority than John McEnroe said it is not a sport if you do not have to run. How could it be a sport or a game if you don't even have to change clothes. People play golf because they can't kick the habit. From my experience and what my friends have told me, golf produces many of the same effects as drug addiction.

For one thing, it often leaves one terribly hung over. There is the throbbing headache from over-taxing the brain with trying to devise a creative way to justify the reduction of the number six to a four. We find that, like alcohol or drugs, golf causes us to be a bit slipshod in our record keeping. It is so easy to forget that shot with the four iron that sent the divot farther than the ball. Other shots we tend to forget: 1) the whiff on the tee box; 2) the fairway shot that topped the ball and bounced it straight up in the air; 3) the fourth, fifth and sixth shot that left the ball in the sand trap two inches from its original position; and 4) the beautiful 150 yard seven iron that required 155 yards to carry the water hazard.

Like most addictions, golf is expensive. The implements of the game are simple to a fault. Eight slender clubs whose striking surface is bent upward in varying degrees. Allegedly, this allows the golfer (I won't use the word player here. That implies a participant in a game.) to vary the loft and the distance which the ball will travel when well struck with one of these simple instruments. That is a ploy to have you believe there is something scientific about this endeavor and that you actually have some control over the outcome of same. Nothing could be further from the truth. These eight clubs are accompanied by something called woods which are, today, not woods at all. They are actually elongated steel-titanium-magnesium-ceramic-molybdenum alloy instruments which are supposed to give the ball a ride of some distance off the tee or fairway. In addition there is a small tool about the length of an old jack handle, called a putter. With it, one is supposed to putt (hit a short stroke, I think) the ball into the hole. Any one of these clubs could set you back the price of a house payment. I am told, that, as with cocaine, it is possible to spend just about any amount one might choose on golf equipment. And like cocaine, once you start buying, there seems to be an uncontrollable urge to have more of it, bigger, better and more technologically pure.

The cost of the golf balls is another matter completely. Again, it is possible to pay anywhere from $18.00 a dozen to about $40.00 a dozen. No matter the cost, some golf balls are bound to find the water hazard and the woods. There are times when it seems they are so drawn to these targets that makers of Patriot missiles and smart bombs should delve into the guidance system installed in these balls. The point of it, of course, is to help you lose as many as possible. How on earth do you think equipment manufacturing companies manage to pay obscene endorsements to the golfers, not players, who use them and advertise same on every stitch of clothing they wear in front of a television camera.

Golf, as with so many addictions, leaves one feeling guilty and remorseful. We steal time away from our loved ones to feed our addiction. We rationalize spending the grocery money on cart fees. We go into deep denial and tell ourselves we can go out and hit a bucket of balls at the driving range and quit any time we want. We kid ourselves that we can take a few practice swings with that "new and improved" Big Momma-Space Age-Double Whammy-Out of Sight-Tiger Woods endorsed driver without plunking down the one-time only sale price of $500.00.

It is impossible for an addict to be honest. This is perhaps the clinching argument that golf is an addiction. The addict lies about how much he uses. He lies about how often he uses. He denies the time he spends looking for his next drink or fix.

Except on publicly documented occasions, such as televised tournaments, golfers lie about almost every aspect of their addiction. If you are a duffer and haven't established a handicap, you will take a number of strokes off your real score. Nobody shoots more than a 95, even though he may have lost six balls during the round. If you are an experienced golfer and have established a handicap, you always 'sandbag' (add a few strokes) your score to give you the best possible handicap for the next club tournament. Assuming you are joining a group for a "friendly" (no such thing) round of golf, you will report that you haven't played for weeks when clearly the calluses on your hands indicate you have played at least 18 holes a day for the past three weeks.

I think you get the picture. Golf takes control of your life, just as cigarettes, alcohol or drugs are prone to do. The golfer who can go out, hit a bucket of balls or play a round of golf (See, it isn't even called a 'game' or a 'match'. It is called a *round*.) and walk away without feeling bad about himself, or lying about it, or having a guilt hangover, or planning his next outing, is not really a golfer. HE IS A TENNIS PLAYER.

The Top of Colorado

I have had an itch I wanted to scratch for the last five years or so.

We have spent our summers in Colorado for the past 10 years. Hiking, along with cycling and tennis, has been one of our favorite activities. A few years ago, at the urging of my brother-in-law, I joined him to hike Quandary Peak, one of Colorado's 54 *fourteeners*, (exceeds 14,000-foot elevation). It was a lung-busting, knee-aching struggle to reach the 14,265-foot summit, especially since I had been in Colorado for only seven days. The hiking distance was three miles, one way, with an elevation gain of 3,370 feet.

A couple years later, a friend and I decided to do Democrat Peak, not because of its political implications, but because of its accessibility. It is 14,148 feet above sea level and is a climb of about 3 miles hiking distance and 2,150 feet elevation gain.

One would think that struggling up those peaks would provide enough physical pain, mental doubt and emotional humiliation to satisfy a 76 + year-old man for the rest of his life. But, the itch remained.

The itch was Mount Elbert, at 14,433 feet, the tallest of the 54 Colorado fourteeners. It lies—or rises—about 15 miles south of Leadville and is easily accessible from our temporary residence in Summit County. Recently, I was discussing hiking possibilities with Jim Odom, a neighbor and friend, who is an accomplished hiker. I, with more bravado than intelligence, mentioned that I had always wanted to climb Mount Elbert. He grabbed that suggestion like a hungry dog on a butcher-shop bone.

Shortly, we were organizing a hike with two other part-time Colorado residents, Hank Mol and Hank Kreis.

Since it would be a 50-mile drive to the trailhead and the likelihood of afternoon showers and thunderstorms is always a concern, we agreed an early start was essential. We wanted to be on the trail by 6:30 a.m. That meant a 4:00 a.m. wake-up.

We made the drive and managed to enter the trailhead by 6:20 on the morning of July 30th. The temperature was in the mid-30s at the 9,600-foot elevation trailhead. Anticipating a mountain sunrise that would bring the temperature to the mid-70s, I declined donning my jacket as we set out in teeth-chattering weather and with anxiety induced enthusiasm.

The first two miles of the six-mile climb were along a dirt road. A 4-wheel drive vehicle with a high clearance is required on that road. We did not have one. The ascent was gentle and it was a relatively easy hike to the actual beginning of the assault on Mount Elbert.

Our enthusiasm, fueled by the frosty morning and undaunted by ignorance of what lay ahead, took us up the initial climb through a pristine forest of lodge-pole pines and groves of dancing aspen. At around 12,000 feet, and some four miles into the hike, we reached the tree line, still eager and determined, but with less conversation among the four of us. We passed groups and exchanged pleasantries—Where you from? You going all the way up? Have you hiked Elbert before? Groups passed us and we took pictures. To that point it was a bit of a party atmosphere and in spite of the steep trail, our anticipation kept us pushing forward with enthusiasm.

Once we climbed above the tree line, the trail became a rocky climb, ambling across ever-ascending ridges and dipping occasionally to a depression, which offered no relief from the relentless resistance of the uphill grade. The wide-open landscape offered a somewhat disturbing perspective on what lay ahead. We could see for at least a half-mile, but what we saw was more of what we were struggling with at the moment—a narrow rocky trail, with occasional switchbacks. Ant-sized humans, engaged in the same struggle we were, inhabited the trail.

I measured my progress by the difficulty of my breathing. At 13,000-foot, it is apparent, even to Toto, that we are no longer in Kansas. It is impossible to sip water while walking at that altitude. I was able to keep hiking for prolonged periods until I approached the 14,000-foot level. At that altitude, I could only negotiate approximately 50 yards without stopping for air. The only thing that kept me going was my knowing that

Jim and Hank Kreis were ahead of me and that Kreis had actually arrived at the summit.

After a five-hour struggle, I rounded a switchback to see the flat wind-blown top of Mount Elbert. A simple aged-to-gray pine pole about 4 inches in diameter marked the official summit. And at that moment, that was the most beautiful piece of wood in the world. I had covered about six miles and had climbed 4,800 feet.

In addition to the pine pole, there were 30 to 40 other climbers occupying the summit. Among them was a fellow Aggie, class of '05, now living in Colorado. We took a picture giving the "Gig 'Em" sign. But the most interesting and unusual occurrence was the fellow, in a tux shirt and tie, proposing to his fiancé who, upon reaching the summit, had donned a dress over her hiking shorts. If they can endure climbing Mount Elbert, they should manage the travails of marriage with no problems.

The trip down was an uneventful four hours that sapped the last bit of strength and energy we had.

Was it worth it? Of course. That itch has been scratched.

The Joy of Cycling

There is exceptional joy in cycling if one can accept that fatigue, pain, thirst, hunger, and monotony are joyful. As one approaches the notion of propelling oneself along an asphalt highway at what is now considered a snail's pace, one must resolve that patience and effort will be the order of the day. Even the best of cyclists, i.e., the professionals, who can attain speeds of 30 miles per hour, and average speeds of 25 miles per hour, for 100 miles or more are traveling at a snail's pace when compared to a 4,000 pound plus, behemoth, capable of exceeding 100 miles per hour and demands only the pressure of one's foot, or the even less demanding setting of the cruise control.

But, what satisfaction is gained from cocooning in an air-conditioned compartment and hurtling down the road at those speeds? Where is the feel of the breeze that cools your body by evaporating the sweat on you back, as you say a small prayer of thanks for nature's kindness?

As the miles unfold, the stress on the back and shoulders tells you that your entire body is involved in the effort. Yes, it is your legs that are moving, applying pressure on the pedals as they rotate and transfer the energy to the wheels of the bike. But the arms and shoulders keep the wheel on the desired path and allow the mind to select the route.

Road-kill occasionally fills the nostrils and vultures circle in ballet-like patterns, assessing the prize and alerting others of their ilk to the awaiting feast. They grudgingly give ground as you approach, but only as much as they think will keep them safe from that ill-dressed predator approaching on that impossible two-wheeled machine. The vulture exhibits his attitude toward the temporary intruder as he issues an audible squawk and promptly turns back to the road-kill. To him, the cyclist is a non-entity. The week-old venison is of much greater concern.

Stretches of the route will be filled with solitude. That is when you tune in to the rhythm of the tires and compare it with your own body rhythm as your legs mechanically rotate and energize the rest of your body parts. Daydreams form. You are no longer on Frances Harris Road, headed to Old Bastrop Highway, you are in the peloton, headed for the French Alps, as you pace yourself for the long grueling days of the rest of the Tour de France. Lance is just ahead of you and will probably do a break-away within the next mile or so.

The down-hill stretch is about a half-mile ahead. A great opportunity to reach for a personal best. With a mild breeze at your back and clear sailing for the half-mile descent, 40 miles per hour should be possible. To be safe, you know to keep your eyes on the road, not the speedometer, you pump your legs as fast as possible. You can check speed at the bottom of the hill. Didn't make it. Not to worry, there'll be another ride another day…with a better wind.

Here's the hill we all hate. It's over a quarter mile up and five miles an hour, for you, is about the best you can do. The legs burn. Your breath comes from labored lungs. Doubt creeps in. Will you make it? The pedals are almost impossible to rotate, but to let up is to fail. (*Pain is temporary, quitting is forever:* Lance Armstrong). And, failing is not an option. Just as the lungs have reached capacity and the legs are one solid burn, the pedal goes down a little easier; the rise becomes less steep; there is slight respite; and relief washes over you like a waterfall. The rest is easy.

After a congratulatory mile or so, you begin to notice the condition of the road. The potholes that the 4,000 pound behemoth glides over with ease, grab your one-inch wide tire and bounce you off the bike seat. It rattles your bones slightly, but it's just something you notice on a bike. Your tires are pumped to 120 pounds per square inch of pressure. The smallest pebble under that tire rattles your teeth. So, you get to know the grit and grain of the area over which you ride.

The odometer hits 20 miles, but you don't notice. The lungs are in a rhythm; the legs are rotating the pedals at a comfortable pace; the sky is a little bluer; the breeze is cooler; there is a familiar smoothness to your movement. Effortless. You move along, hearing, but not hearing the mocking bird on the fence; you are in your world and you create the environment. Contentment and pride of achievement mingle with daydreams, memories, and the sudden sound of Willie's gravelly voice and sad lyrics, "Angels flying too close to the ground...." Five miles later the finish looms and you realize what a joy it has been. The bike seems to relax and signals you to do the same. Another time with yourself, bonding with nature, living the dream; sorting it all out; letting go of useless; analyzing the useful. The joy of cycling.

Cycling—at Any Age

As I write this, the Tour de France is underway and it hardly makes a blip on the screen of American sports enthusiasts. By the time you read this, the Tour will be in the American dust bin of sporting events.

We Americans have little interest in the Tour de France, perhaps the most demanding of all major sporting events. The two most prominent Americans riding this year are George Hincappie and Levi Leipheimer. Ever heard of them? No.

We don't ride bikes after the age of 10. Oh, there are a few of us who toss aside our embarrassment and think about dusting off the old Raleigh ten-speed and taking a whirl around the block. But by the time we reach middle age, golf and tennis have become much more respectable pursuits and in spite of our inability to master either, we find ourselves enduring the busted knees of tennis or the utter frustrations of the unpredictability of our golf game.

Having grown tired of the crippling effects of tennis and the emotional rollercoaster of golf, I purchased a bicycle two months before my 70th birthday. That was in September 2001. It was a 21 speed mountain bike. Since the plan was to ride it around town; run a few errands; and do a few five mile exercise rides, I had the bike shop replace the knobby tires with smoother, smaller ones.

In the course of the next few weeks, I joined a couple of my friends in their weekly 15 mile ride along the back roads of Hays, Guadalupe, and Comal Counties. It was pleasant and easy enough and yet, provided a reasonable body and aerobic workout. Next thing I know I'm riding through cattle-guards and over dirt roads from San Marcos to Wimberley.

One of those aforementioned friends collared me one day and pointed to a brochure advertising the '*most beautiful bike ride in the world.*' It was a 100 mile ride around Lake Tahoe, Nevada to raise funds for the Lymphoma-Leukemia Society. We signed up to do the ride, only to discover that to qualify, we had to raise $3,000.00 each.

I had trepidations about doing a 100 mile ride and so, I was somewhat relieved by the fund-raising requirement. I never imagined I could raise that much money. After sending letters of solicitation to about 100 of my closest friends, the first response I opened contained a check for $1,000.00.

I began training with an Austin group. It didn't take long for me to discover my mountain bike, even with the slick tires was not the answer to a100 mile ride. We began with 20 and 25 mile routes on the weekends. Soon, the routes became 30 to 35 miles. Then they became 75 to 80 miles. I learned the meaning of endurance and determination.

As a result of the training and camaraderie, I became hooked on cycling. My knees improved to the point that I could, once again, play tennis without pain and my aerobics were better than when I ran four miles a day. But with my heavy, steel-framed mountain bike, I was always bringing up the rear.

I was lucky enough to find a used road bike in excellent condition for $500.00. I caution the novice here. Even if you were the best in your class on the Schwinn at age 10, you will need to do some refresher riding to master the road bike. Pedal clips and the sharp turning radius require familiarization. The road bike weighs about 20 pounds, has up to 30 speeds, and only about a half inch of tire surface is in contact with the ground.

My original road bike was an aluminum frame with 27 speeds. I have since purchased a carbon fiber bike with 30 speeds. The carbon fiber frame rides somewhat smoother and is generally a few pounds lighter.

Before you head to the shop to purchase your first bike, be aware that there are as many options to purchasing a bicycle as when considering a new car, i.e., what kind of frame is best for you? Hint: if you are a 280 pound Clydesdale, you probably don't want carbon fiber. So, as with an automobile, consider what purpose the bike will serve. If you have doubts about where to begin, an expert at any bike shop will steer you in the right direction.

Following my own advice, I visited Tamara at Pedal Power and role-played the innocent new cyclist. Here's what I learned:

Query: I am uncertain where this is going. I just want to try cycling for exercise.

Answer: Go with the hybrid. It's more comfortable, more versatile and more affordable.

Q: Affordable? How affordable?

A. You can start around $400.00, but real value is going to be from $500.00 to $600.00

Q: What's the difference between your bikes and those in the big box stores?

A. Besides the quality, theirs come in only one size. We fit the bike to the rider for safety, comfort, and endurance riding.

Q: What do you mean size?

A: Basically, I'm referring to the frame size. This bike comes in 15 inch, 17 inch, 20 inch and 22 inch size. This fact alone affects, knees, back, and comfort of the rider.

We discussed many more aspects of cycling and choosing a bike, but space limitation precludes including the full interview, but you get the picture.

In addition to the Lake Tahoe ride, I have since ridden three MS 150s; numerous charity rides, ranging from 60+ to 100 miles. During the summer, I ride the mountain trails in Summit County, Colorado. I have about 12,000 miles on the road bike I purchased in September 2006. I try to do 50 to 70 miles a week.

Cycling is a lifetime sport. I will have my 80th birthday, November 12th and I anticipate riding at least 80 miles that week.

The First Wurst Bike Ride of Texas

We live in an age when people increasingly refuse to act their age. The young (or many of them) yearn to be older, while the older (or many of them) yearn to be younger. We have progressively demolished the life cycle's traditional stages.... Middle age which once arrived in the mid-30's or early 40's has been pushed well back beyond 50 or even 60. As for old age, it is rarely mentioned until the paraphernalia of physical decay (canes, walkers, wheelchairs) make it moot. Robert J. Samuelson in November 3, 2003 issue of Newsweek Magazine.

I had no idea I was part of a trend until I read the above excerpt from Newsweek.

I have certainly never been trendy. I have clothes in my closet from the 70's. I still haven't mastered interjecting "like" before every phrase I utter; and I would rather listen to an auctioneer sell furniture than to hear an Em 'N Em CD.

I began to think I was into the paraphernalia of old age when I had to trade my running shoes for a bicycle. About two years ago, I took up cycling, and I believe Dierks Bentley wrote his new country song, "What Was I Thinkn'?" with me in mind.

My latest excursion into Dizzyland was riding the Wurst Bike Ride in Texas.

It was held November 1st, just 12 days before my 72d. birthday. It would go from Austin to New Braunfels, over a distance of 66 miles.

I was attracted to the ride because it was near-by; it was less than 100 miles; it cost only $30.00 to participate; and since it was the first time the event had been held, there would not be a horde (Lance's Ride for the Roses attracted 5,500 riders) of riders.

The real attraction, however, was that it would end at Landa Park in New Braunfels where Wurst Fest would be underway. There was also a notation that there would be an ample supply of Fat Tire at the end of the ride. Those of you who fancy yourselves connoisseurs of beer know that Fat Tire does not fit a bicycle wheel.

We got underway at 8:20 AM. On-site registration took a little longer than anticipated. Two hundred dedicated cyclists pedaled along McKinney Falls Parkway, headed for Creedmore, our first rest stop. An hour later and 12 or 13 miles on the bike and the crowd at the rest stop doubled the population (211) of Creedmore.

We traversed some of the more scenic back roads of Travis, Caldwell, Hays and Comal County. When one travels IH-35 or some of the larger state and county roads, it is easy to forget or ignore that less than a mile on the left or right, there are narrow two-lane roads separating verdant fields and pastures populated by bucolic Angus, Herefords, or mixed breeds.

The surface of these roads may be less than glassy smooth, but one can hear clearly a crow's caw or observe a possum safely wig wag his way across the asphalt. In the open air, one has the chance to inhale the pungent odor of the decaying corpse of a deer or the unmistakable calling card of an excited skunk, sensual phenomena we rarely experience as we speed down the interstate, encapsulated in our climate-controlled behemoths.

The ubiquitous vultures, circle in search of carrion or road kill. If they are feeding alongside the road, they often refuse to fly as the bicycles approach.

The second rest stop is another 12 or 13 miles. By now pain starts to inch its way across my shoulders and there is a slight reminder that I have a strained groin muscle from an earlier ride. A short break and the pain seems to disappear. Though the weather is near perfect, I remind myself to drink lots of liquids and stay stoked with fruit and pretzels.

The third rest stop is in Maxwell, some 35 miles into the ride. At this point, I have begun to notice changes in the landscape. Those verdant pastures are now populated by double-wides, which, it appears, will soon be replaced by KB Homes. I have also begun to notice I'm counting the miles to Landa Park. I tell myself two 15 mile segments are much easier than another 30 miles. Cyclists often need some sort of self-deception to get through the day.

County lines become apparent because the highways in Hays County are easily the least bicycle friendly of all the four counties encountered.

However, Hays County Sheriff's Department provided excellent support along Highway 80 and other high density traffic areas. They were friendly, safety-conscious, and courteous. Motorists, in general, had a similar attitude, even when there was no traffic control. Only once did I get a horn blast from a disgruntled driver.

From Maxwell we made our way to Martindale where we crossed the San Marcos River and headed for Old Bastrop Road, a familiar route to many San Marcos cyclists. Old Bastrop Road took us to the fourth rest stop at the Watson Lane /IH-35 intersection.

The pain in my shoulders went all the way to my ankles, but after coming this far, what the heck? Besides the Fat Tire must be getting cold.

The most difficult traffic along the route was from Watson Lane into Gruene, and with the finish only a few miles away, extreme caution was the answer.

I entered Landa Park, greeted by quizzical stares of Wurst Fest goers, but the beauty of the Comal River, the shade created by the huge oaks and the anticipation of the cold Fat Tire absorbed all the pain in my body.

The Wurst Ride of Texas, of which this was the first, benefits the Lone Star Paralysis Foundation. I plan to refuse to act my age again next year with the Second Wurst Ride of Texas. Anticipate it will be much larger.

Cycling Club

There has to be a chromosome somewhere in my makeup with a bundle of Don Quixote genes. Two months ago, after repeatedly hearing from many of the people with whom I ride that San Marcos needs a bicycle club, I said to myself, "Self, why don't you organize a bike club?" At that point, the DQ genes kicked in and said, "Yes. Why not pursue the *Impossible Dream*. So, I sent an email to a whole bunch of cyclists on my email list and I pounded out a 750 word justification for my pathologically optimistic dream of organizing a group of cyclists here in San Marcos. The thought was that we might accomplish whatever it is that special interest clubs accomplish, i.e., organize rides, lobby for a bicycle friendly San Marcos, bring together people with a common interest, socialize, make bicycles more visible in San Marcos, and promote healthy living through cycling.

OK, we need a unifying document. As you know I am research-challenged. Google, this millennium's Encyclopedia Britannica, led me to the constitution and bylaws of the San Marcos Runners Club, which I shamelessly copied. With the aid and encouragement of the Parks and Recreation Department, I announced the inaugural meeting for March 10th at the Activity Center.

Twenty people attended and we got absolutely nothing done. Well, that's not quite right. I passed out copies of the San Marcos Runner's Club constitution and bylaws and told those present to read it. I got more email addresses. And, we decided to have another meeting.

The April 6th meeting was less well attended. Ten hardy souls made time to attend the meeting and pay the $10.00 dues. I got a couple more e-mail addresses. But, we conducted business anyway.

The agenda included adopting a constitution and electing officers. We adopted the constitution. No officers were elected because there were not enough people to nominate. Many of those who attended are already involved with other boards, committees, clubs, or community organizations. One member suggested that my announcement that the purpose of the meeting was to collect dues and elect officers was a guarantee of poor attendance. In fact, he suggested that getting 10 people to the meeting was encouraging.

Cyclists are, by nature, a somewhat independent, eccentric, ego-driven, masochistic bunch of misfits with a skewed sense of values. How many of you sane people would sit for three hours, on a four-inch wide seat, in a hunched-over position that causes excruciating shoulder pain, just to get some exercise. Further, how many of you would pay from $3,000.00 to $5,000.00 for a toy similar to the one you abandoned when you were 10 years old because you were too mature for bike-riding?

There are all sorts of ego manifestations among cyclists. One, of course is the average speed for a 30 to 40 mile ride. There's the 12-15 mph crowd and then there's the 17-20 mph crowd. Ne'er the twain shall meet. In addition, there's the two-ring versus the three-ring front crank crowd. Three rings are considered amateur.

Cycling has its share of fetish worshipers. Heart monitors are essential for some. Others never ride without a computer to measure trip distance, current speed, average speed, and total distance. Some riders in the mountains insist on an altimeter. What I would like is a gadget that measures wind speed. A given in cycling is that no matter which direction one travels, it is always into the wind.

I have discovered that trying to organize a cycling club is similar to herding cats, or nailing Jell-O to the wall. And, about the time I'm ready to give up, someone activates my pathological optimism by complimenting me on my efforts and reaffirming for me how badly San Marcos needs a cycling club.

So, May 4th at 6:30 p.m., the third meeting of the San Marcos Cycling Club will meet in the general purpose room of the San Marcos Activity Center. We will elect officers and collect dues ($10.00 for the year). We might even plan a ride. But first, you *cats* have to consent to be herded into an organization with a purpose. So, show up, you might meet someone. *Results: The Cyclist Club faltered for lack of participation and one should know that organizing cyclists is similar to herding cats.*

Cycling for the Scroogeous*

*Author's Note: Scroogeos is a word coined by the author. From Dickens' A Christmas Carol—the mashup of Scrooge and frugal/thrifty/et.al

With the price of gasoline rapidly approaching three dollars a gallon and forecasts suggesting it will go higher and stay that way for several years, it seems a good time to suggest a partial solution to the problem.

Hydrogen cars are years in the future. Hybrid cars are so expensive they hardly represent a saving. Walking would help, but it is awfully slow and is a terrible waste of the asphalt we have so diligently spread over the past 60 years. The answer is:

BICYCLES!!!!

Those of you who know my prejudices are not surprised. There are no zealots like a converted zealot, as they say about people who experience a religious conversion. They can often be a Johnny-one-note, pestering, boring, intolerant, cock-sure, arrogant, holier-than-thou and a genuine pain-in-the-neck nut case. People have likened me to all of the above as I preached my gospel of cycling.

No doubt, many quit reading this article at the word "bicycles," but for those whose curiosity got you this far, thanks.

In September 2001, I was on the verge of my 70th birthday, when I had the urge of a 10 year-old for a bicycle. I suppose it's true that as we age, we return to our childish ways. With memories of purchasing my first two-wheeler (used) for $10.00, I visited a local bike shop determined to get a really good bicycle. I was prepared to spend as much as $75. As I priced the shiny samples of rolling stock, I found I could not buy a frame for that price, much less a complete bicycle.

Since price was a factor at that time and I had no idea what kind of bike I really wanted, I spent an inordinate amount of time shopping. Highly unusual for the guy who tries on a pair of shoes and if they fit, walks out the store. Nevertheless, my urge for a bicycle outweighed my pinch-penny budgeting habits and I selected a basic mountain bike and put smaller, slicker tires on it to accommodate my intentions of riding to the gym, post office, and barber shop.

Then, I needed a rack to carry small cargo, extra reflectors for safety, a lock, a helmet, gloves, toe-clips, a computer to clock my speed and mileage. I got my under-$300 basic bike out of the store for just over $400.

Today's bicycle is not yesteryear's one-speed Raleigh with a thumb-operated bell and a built-in headlight on the front fender, chain-guards and a kick-stand. It is not even yesterday's 10-speed Schwinn. The $400 bike has 21 speeds, front shocks, hand brakes, and a special alloy frame.

The fun was just beginning. I tooled around town for a couple of months, learning to ride this new contraption. And one does need to re-learn. As mentioned, it is not your old one-speed Raleigh. I took a number of spills which hurt nothing but my ego. Through a series of unlikely circumstances, I was enticed to enter a 100 mile ride to be held at Lake Tahoe, Nevada in June, 2002. I had no idea.

In January, 2002, I began training with a group in Austin. I soon learned how little I knew about cycling. I showed up in a cotton T-shirt, cotton shorts and tennis shoes for my first few rides. I was as out of place as Pee Wee Herman at a power-lifting contest. I discovered there is a regular Chinese menu of bicycle sizes, types, shapes, brands, and options. Also, there are cycling pants, cycling shirts and cycling shoes and socks. But, the basic difference between me and the rest of the people headed for Lake Tahoe was my mountain bike versus their road bikes.

A road bike has tires just larger than a pencil, handlebars that don't really let you handle, and shoe clips that will not let go when you are trying to dismount. It weighs about 18 pounds, has 27 speeds, and the smallest bit of gravel or loose surface will put you face down on the asphalt before you know you are falling.

I did get a road bike; I did get some cycling clothes; I did ride the 100 mile Lake Tahoe ride; I did become addicted to cycling.

If you have stayed with me this far, you might wonder if I'm promoting or denigrating cycling. I provided the preamble in the interest of full disclosure. However, cycling does not have to be as complicated as I made it. It can be as simple and easy as I originally planned. And that is a major reason for getting a bicycle.

So you spend $400. You can spend less. Or if you are now driving a Beamer, you can put $2500 into a mid-range bike and maintain your status.

It is amazing how rapidly one can put mileage on a bicycle. Without being a diligent bicycle traveler, I easily put 100 miles a month, going to the gym, the post office, the barber shop and running other errands. One of my greatest pleasures is cycling to my doctors' appointments. I dare them to ask if I'm getting any exercise.

At bike speed, you can appreciate the outdoors. When was the last time you felt the wind in your face, the sun on your back and a few bumps in the road? When was the last time you extended your physical exertion for more than 15 minutes? OK, all you smirking joggers out there, I have two words for you—KNEE JOINTS. Cycling is low impact with a marvelous aerobic effect.

Further, there is a smorgasbord of road-kill scents out there that never permeate the air-conditioned capsule of your 4,000 pound SUV.

If half the students at Texas State (13,000) traded cars for bicycles, what would that do to San Marcos traffic? What if the administration gave a $10 an hour tuition discount to all students who brought bicycles instead of cars? Think of the parking requirement that would eliminate. I stole that idea, by the way.

I have heard all the arguments about cycling dangers. I have heard a number of stories about people getting hurt while riding. I have read the Austin American-Statesman's account of Austin's latest cycling fatality. San Marcos and Hays County are not particularly bicycle-friendly at the infra-structure level, but on the road, individual drivers are exceptionally courteous. Many drivers will linger at STOP signs to let me through. They make every effort to give me plenty of room when passing. I try to acknowledge a motorist's concern and I try to return the favor by riding cautiously and courteously—and I would hope all local cyclists do the same.

I suppose it is time to get off my soap box, but before I do, think what San Marcos might look like if half the students adopted the bicycle rather than the car, and one-fourth the citizens who are able, biked where feasible for one month.

Just for once, listen to the 10 year-old in you. Probably would not bring down the price of gasoline, but it might eliminate the 5:00 o'clock line of cars that backs up on Hopkins Street from I-H 35 to the library.

MS 150—2008

After climbing Mount Elbert, the highest of the 54 fourteeners in Colorado, this summer, I decided to refrain from such foolishness for awhile. But, I guess I'm a sucker for punishment and... a pretty face... or two.

Before I left for Colorado this summer, there was talk among Mary Braun, Lauren Lamm-Sorell, and me about doing the MS (multiple sclerosis) 150, a bike ride from San Antonio to Corpus Christi that covers about 160 miles and requires two days riding. The first day ride is officially 96.4 miles.

Upon my return from Colorado, I discovered, somewhat to my chagrin, that Mary and Lauren had not forgotten our earlier discussion. While I rode a great deal in Colorado, I wasn't sure I wanted to put myself through the excruciating misery that kind of ride entails. However, being a sucker for a pretty face, and having been reassured that their mates, Jason Braun and Marty Sorell would be nearby with drink, sustenance, medical supplies, and a bicycle repair kit, I hid my fears and agreed to undertake the trip. In addition, I was assured that there would be no sleeping on the ground in a tent.

We spent the night of October 3d in rather plush quarters at Fort Sam in San Antonio. The next morning, we pulled our lethargic bodies out of bed at 5:00 a.m., washed down a bran muffin or two with motel coffee and found our way to the start-line at the AT&T Center parking lot.

Around 7:45 a.m. we found ourselves, along with 3,500 other braver than bright souls, herded toward a so-called starting line. This process took us about 30 minutes, but by shortly after 8:00 a.m., we were underway to our day's destination of Beeville.

There is always an adrenaline rush at the beginning of these rides. And the start is usually smooth and flat. So, for the first hour or so, one feels as if he/she might be able to do 18 mph all day. It is easy to bypass the first rest stop, normally at around the 10 to 12 mile marker. As one glides by the tyros who are doing the ride because they're with a buddy, or they want to see if they can do it, or they've been goaded into making the effort, or this seems like a good way to lose some weight, one feels an inner sense of superiority and just a touch of snobbery as the memory calls up the inconvenience and the discomfort of the 30 and 40 mile training rides.

On this particular ride, the hills are rather benign—at least compared to those on the mountain rides I was doing in Colorado— but the headwind tends to make up for the inclines. Early, the breezes were soft and cool and the self-generated wind aided in evaporating the perspiration. This had an added cooling effect.

As the morning wore on, the sun cut through the clouds and made its presence felt. The warming effect stirred the winds and by noon, there was a noticeable resistance confronting us from the south. After riding some 50 plus miles, consuming a whole bunch of bananas (well, not literally), eating orange slices, drinking Gatorade and water, and trying to find a comfortable position on that miniscule bike seat, Falls City, site of the lunch break, was a delightful sight. Ham, turkey, and peanut butter and jelly sandwiches were most welcome. But even more welcome was the relief from the constant pedaling, the shoulder cramps, and the hard seat.

After a 45 minute break and some real food, we were on our way again. From Falls City to about 10 miles from Beeville, we not only encountered a stronger headwind, the road, especially the shoulder, was wash-board rough. Large pebbles and marble size gravel made riding much more difficult and tiring than normal. Road bikes have about a half-inch of tire surface that actually contacts the road and the tires are inflated at 100 to 120 pounds of pressure. Every ripple in the road is transferred to the body of the rider. Try to imagine climbing a ladder for three hours while the bottom of it is hooked to a steadily pounding jackhammer.

About 10 hours later, eight of which were spent on that miniscule seat, I arrived in Beeville, some 96.4 miles from San Antonio.

Tired, hungry, dehydrated, sore, windblown, and did I mention *tired*, we set off for dinner in Mathis. At Santiago's restaurant, I ordered the largest combination plate on the menu. Hunger beat exhaustion and I finished the meal before I fell asleep.

At this point, we had to find our overnight quarters. After some guessing and back-tracking, we came upon the mobile home where we were to spend the night. I'll simply describe it as the most bachelor of bachelor households. That really did not matter. We could have slept on rocks.

On Sunday, we once again got up before the sun and headed to the start line in Beeville where we met up with Josh and Callie Swindle of San Marcos. To get a jump on the crowd, we took off around 7:30 a.m., and once again, we were seduced by the calm breeze, the cool ambience and the smooth road. Josh, an excellent rider, left us in his wake. I managed to hang with Callie for about 12 miles before the sun and the wind began to influence our progress. At that point, my 76 year-old legs could no longer make up for the 50 + years of difference and she dropped me like a hot rock.

I often could manage only about eight miles an hour as I came nearer to Corpus Christi Bay.

After grinding out about 45 miles, Mary, Lauren and I met at Portland, the last rest stop. We rode the last 10 miles together and made it across the Bay Bridge, around 1:00 p.m. The bridge is another matter. It reminded me of my climbs up Ute Pass in Summit County, Colorado, but it was less than a mile, so the burn, the ache, the cramp, and the exhaustion were put aside for a short while as we inched our way across the bridge to the finish line.

I did all this six weeks before my 77th birthday. I swear I'm going to quit this foolishness when I'm 80...I think! bibb111231@yahoo.com.

The Wurst Ride in Texas—3d edition

November 11th was Veterans Day and the day before my 75th birthday. It was a cold day for Texas, about 45 degrees, when I awoke at 5:00 AM to don that silly costume cyclists wear. The spandex shorts, the lycra top with the pockets in the back and that god-awful helmet make one look a lot like a land-locked scuba diver. Strangely enough, that outfit is genuinely utilitarian.

The pants are designed to fit snugly, to allow maximum freedom of movement for the legs and to avoid catching or snagging on a stray object of any sort. They are short, to allow the legs to cool and to prevent fouling the bicycle chain.

The shirt is made of a material that wicks perspiration from the body and enhances evaporation, aiding in cooling the upper torso. It has pockets in the back where it is easy to carry items without back strain. They hold whatever one puts in them, but I put my wallet, keys, glasses, nose wipes, and power bars and cell phone in them. You can reach them easily while riding.

That ugly helmet is essential. It is made of a light weight material, much like Styrofoam and has minimum padding inside. It has slots all across the top to provide cooling for the rider. It is much lighter than it looks and that is good because on a road bike, one rides in a bit of a crouch which requires you to lift your head. That puts some strain on your neck and shoulders. The helmet is effective as a safety device. No matter your skills, a fall is awaiting the best of riders at the next gravel-strewn corner, the next railroad track, or the next rain-slick slice of highway. The helmet often prevents a concussion or worse.

Each piece of the equipment I described above can cost from $20.00 to $120.00.

At 6:30 my friend, Luke and my neighbor (and friend) Lori and I loaded our bikes in Luke's truck and headed for Austin, to participate in the third rendition of the Wurst Ride in Texas. It begins just outside McKinney State Park on Highway 71 and meanders through the countryside all the way to Landa Park in New Braunfels, a distance of 60 miles. About 600 cyclists participated.

This year would be different from last year's ride. The route is on a southerly heading almost all the way. Last year, the wind was from the south at speeds of approximately 20 miles per hour. Wind resistance is the most difficult obstacle for a cyclist because it is constant and often makes balance an issue. There is no relaxing in a wind of that speed. There were higher gusts on occasion.

This is my third year to participate in the event and it was a breeze. Pun intended. The wind was out of the north at about 15 mph and that moves the cyclist along at a good clip without a tremendous effort. It is easy to fantasize that your riding has improved immensely and maybe you really should take up racing. It is even tempting to bypass a few rest stops. As Luke said, "it is almost like cheating."

In a ride of this type, one can identify those who ride a lot. They show up in the gear I described above, and it is usually the high-end brand. Oh, I didn't even mention the special shoes with cleats which can run from $60.00 to $300.00 a pair. They have a bicycle that costs more than you paid for your new car in 1980.

Then there are those who are doing the ride on a dare from someone in the office. They are wearing a pair of cargo shorts, tennis shoes, a Wal-Mart helmet and they are riding a Wal-Mart bike—likely borrowed from the neighbor's 12 year-old. And there are plenty of riders between the elite and the Wal-Mart guy.

One might think the elite riders with the fancy gear and expensive bikes would set themselves apart and have nothing to do with the rider with the borrowed bike. Think again. When the ride starts, we are all in the thing together and if someone has trouble—a flat, a broken chain, a fall—everyone is willing to stop and offer assistance.

Cycling is also gender-neutral. When I first started riding, I didn't have a clue. I began training for a 100 miler with a group in Austin. I was outfitted about like the Wal-Mart guy. When I joined the group for my first training ride, I wondered if I would be able to keep up. Then I saw there were a number of females in the group and I thought, "This will be easy." Was I ever wrong. It took me about a month to get over the fact that every female in the group was going by me as if I were on a stationary bike.

The great thing about bike rides of the Wurst variety is that you travel the back roads, the blue highways, if you will. Very seldom do most of us get off the asphalt strips called interstates or major state highways when traveling. We miss the Creedmores, the Maxwells, the Martindales, and the Gruenes.

We also miss the pungent smell of a dead possum whose carcass is about to become a meal for a turkey vulture. We miss the livestock, the crops, the fence lines and the whole rural scene that once was Texas. We seem to forget that we have farms and ranches where people continue to struggle with the weather and the fluctuation of prices to wrench a living from the soil.

We also forget that not all roads are glassy smooth. When riding in a pneumatically suspended 3,000 pound automobile, all roads seem relatively smooth. When riding an 18 pound bicycle on half-inch tires inflated to 120 pounds of pressure, every pebble, pothole, and ruffle in the roadway registers on your hands, arms, back and most assuredly on your posterior.

All cyclists who participate in rides like the Wurst ride have great respect and appreciation for the numerous volunteers who conduct the ride. First are those who do the registration and administration. Signing up people, getting names, handing out numbers, taking money, and overseeing the whole operation is a volunteer job, requiring people to get up earlier than the cyclists and they stay around long after the last rider has finished. And they have to get other volunteers.

Those who man the rest stops are in place by the time the first rider leaves the start line and remain in place until the last rider passes the particular rest stop. They provide water, bananas, oranges, Gatorade, power bars, band aids and port-o-potties. They also provide sympathy, and encouraging words.

Then there are those who man the Supply and Gear (SAG) vehicles. There is usually at least one bicycle repair expert if you have mechanical difficulties. If you have decided you are not going to finish, but "tell those guys in the office that you did," the SAG will pick you up and take you to the finish line.

The Wurst ride is unique because it is conducted during New Braunfels' celebration of Wurstfest. At the end of the 60-mile ride, there is food along with beer. This year, bratwurst, sausage and sauerkraut along with cold kegs greeted finishers. Last year, the Comal River provided a refreshing dip for some of the riders. This year, that wasn't necessary. It was cool enough without getting in the water.

Finishing a ride of 60 or more miles always gives me a sense of accomplishment. Usually, I'm completely drained—physically and mentally. This year, the ride was easier than usual. I felt better than I could imagine I would. The brats were great and the beer was cold. But, no, I didn't "feel like I cheated."

A Woman I Know

Her San Marcos roots are deeper than Wonder Cave
Her family dates back almost to the Indian braves
Her grandfather came here sometime after the Alamo
One might suppose he had no other place to go

He traded a horse and saddle for some land and the cave
Some say it was the worst deal he ever made
But, like his granddaughter, he was no fool
He bought the springs and made a wonderful pool

Her father, Paul created Aquarena Springs
And even today, the name still rings
Throughout Texas it is a revered landmark
For it was the state's first water park

The young lady certainly played her part
She joined the effort with all her heart
Rest assured it was no small bit she played
She was a well-renowned Aquamaid

As a child she lived in a cabin called *Linger Long*
That could be the title of her song
She's gorgeous; she's great to be around
She's also known as most generous in this town

In San Marcos, she is a well-known BISM
But in her life there is no schism
She is whole and complete; there is no division
She lives her life with a spiritual vision

She is unique; she's special; she is truly one of a kind
To compare with her beauty and charm, no one comes to mind
Our birthday girl is lively; she's smart; she's a lot of fun
And I wish she would tell us how the hell she stays so young

Bibb Underwood
For a Woman I know

My Friend

You are a marvel and a miracle
Unexplainable, beyond understanding
You shed the years
And have no tears that tell us
Of your fears
Are there any?
Of course not
They were expunged long ago
In a place only you would know
And an angel blessed you
And brought long life
And a respite from strife
That you have known
From seeds that were sown
Long ago
For a reason you are here
Sharing the blessings
You were meant to share
With those for whom you care
You live your life
In an open world

Transparent as the perfect pearl
Giving in the shadow of the Lord
Loving and living
Innocent, the little girl
A child that resides inside you
She emerges from the shadows
And refreshes like the morning dew
And known only to a precious few
She is really you

Thanksgiving

This has been an unusual year
It began in deep despair
It ends now without a tear
Because you were there

A lot of little things we did
Made life seem a bit more fair
Our feelings at times we hid
But I knew you were always there

I'm sure we have felt some doubt
But we knew how to care
Even though we wandered about
We learned, together...we've been there

So, I give thanks for your loyalty
You're a queen and a crown you should wear
Because you are truly royalty
And for me you're always there

A Valentine for a Friend

There's a shine, a glow, a PRESENCE
A smile, a feeling that is genuine
A beauty, a spirit that is her essence
A stature, a carriage that is sublime

She's easy to love; easy to know
Exciting and curious and eager to try
She's soft and pure with a perpetual glow
Beneath which, strength, and determination lie

Bright and curious and feeling and caring
She's tough and lively and smart
Her nature is always seeking and daring
It is her soaring spirit that sets her apart

There is only one of her and we are blessed
There is no other with her effervescence
With her, I am completely possessed
She fills all voids with her PRESENCE

2-14-2014

A Birthday

Today is a milestone worth noting
It's your birthday that we celebrate
We know the number but we're not gloating
If we tell, you promised you would decapitate

Suffice to say, you've been here awhile
Always with class and beauty
Of course, you don't always smile
When there are those who shirk their duty

Wishing you a happy day and many more
And since you are hale and hardy
You have many youthful days in store
To raise hell, go crazy and party

An Inspiration from Peak One

Dreams of you are the life of me
And keep me from loneliness
And set me free
To feel your loveliness

Time will give us what we need
As it has done with the Mountain
We may suffer, we may bleed
But, we will find love is a fountain

That is where we will meet and drink
From that place, we will emerge as one
We will begin to feel and cease to think
We will understand the Quest is done

Two Years a Friend

Two years ago we were on a search
For something that seemed
Out of reach

You were seeking something new
And I was trying to hold on
To something old

There were doubts and hurts
And things not known
Unseen and untold

Our life was changing at an unlikely time
And the future seemed uncertain
Yet, there was an aura

To remain upright, I reached for you
And you stood solid and safe
Until I became whole

You made me live in reality
Which I had never done
As we became one

The path is still uncertain
It has a way to go
But we know

We have found that elusive thing
That gives us hope and desire
To keep on living

Life is love and love is you
And the search is ended
At last

Easter 2012

This day was special
And it was you
That made it so

Your love, your caring
And sense of family
Gave it special meaning

There was mutual love;
And respect
And adoration for you

There were expressions
Of feelings
That spoke of love and unity

Your beauty and spirit
Illuminated the day
And renewed all of us

Easter is new beginnings;
You opened your soul
For us to see what can be

This day is imprinted
On my memory in a way
That can not be erased

A Special Day

No matter what you say
It is, after all, your birthday
The years do come and go
But on you, they never show

Presence That Lifts Our Soul

I love you for no reason, but…

As the years go by
They add beauty to
Your countenance
And
Youth to your step
You are a fairy tale
Living and breathing
While
Reality strikes and saps
The less fortunate
You sail through the years
On
Innocence and faith
And living full
A gift to all of us
You
Brighten the days
And part the clouds
And ignite the skies

With
An incandescent smile
That invites and says
Love is my gift
And
We are warmed with hope
As we receive from the depths
Your PRESENCE that lifts
Our soul

Musings for a Friend

I'm here, you're there
What is it that separates us
Space
Is an emptiness that has no
Meaning
Because I'm with you in the
Spirit
And what else is there
When love is the element
Of connectedness
That
Will not be broken
I'm here, you're there
And
We're together as one
But
Separate to test the
Strength of each of us
To
Commit to a feeling without
Obligation
And so, we connect and couple and
Hold tight
And
Then, we let go to
Know
If it is real, if it is love, if it has

Permanence
Then the awareness of
Absence
Fills our being and
We trust in the NOW
To
Guide us to our place
And
To keep us connected by that
Elusive love

She Is…

She is a riddle
Complex
She's an open book
Simple
As a flowing stream
Loving, Giving
Smooth as glass
Powerful
As an ocean storm
Gentle
As a new-born calf
PRESENCE
Fills a room with an aura
Modest
Enough to touch the hem
Innocent
As the baby's first breath
Instinctive
As the hungry wolf
Her spirit
Rides the wind, is in the cloud

She
Is that calm, cool breeze
Touches
Captivates and mystically
She
Owns your soul
And
Shares her own with
You

Marbles and Mud Pies

Her soft dark curls
Hung to her shoulders
And ringed a face
As sweet as taffy candy

He was tow-headed
And berry-brown
Beneath his striped over-alls
His feet peeked out bare as a new-born

Her Mary Janes were black
Over her white stockings
And she wore a floweredy dress
With puffed sleeves

His pockets had marbles
And rocks and a penny he had found
His knuckles were skinned and red
From playing marbles on the ground

She followed him wherever he went
And played marbles with him
Some days she brought jar lids
And they made mud pies

She laughed at him and joined him
When he found mesquite gum
And they chewed it
And made funny faces

She could climb the tallest mesquites
Almost as well as he and she did
But she could not catch
Nor throw a ball so well

Where she came from he did not know
Nor did he ask nor did he care
It only mattered
That she was there

The Pearl and You

You were the simple grain of sand
That began the process
And now you are the Pearl
That radiates many colors
Of beauty and light

There were irritations and
Pains that produced the layers
That formed your
Radiant light and smooth surface
That makes you a precious gem

No Pearl is perfect and
The imperfections make it real
All are the products
Of hurts and failures
Your imperfections are your truth

And so as I gaze upon the
Luminescence that is you
I see the imperfections
Of which you are so aware
And I know my feelings are real

Armistice Day

Author's note: *This article is a departure from what you expect to find in this space. Instead of profiling one person, I have attempted to profile a group of people—more a community, if you will—as they observe Veterans' Day. As the respect for veterans wanes and the significance of the day loses its meaning, I thought it worthwhile to visit the site of my first Armistice Day (Veterans' Day) celebration and share my thoughts and feelings with you.*

I remember the excitement I felt when Armistice Day rolled around. Since before my birth in 1931, Millersview, Texas has celebrated Armistice Day. No one seems to know exactly when it all began. Some thought it might have begun in 1919, but congress did not officially ordain November 11th as a special day until 1926.

I was about 10 years old before I had clear memories of the event. The fact that my birthday fell on the next day played no part in the anticipation. In my family birthdays were not nearly as important as Armistice Day. Next to Christmas, it was the most anticipated day of the year by grown-ups and children alike.

In the late 30's and early 40's Millersview was a typical Texas dryland farm community. In sparsely settled Concho County, Millersview may have consisted of 500 or so families, almost all of which were farmers. My family was an exception. My grandfather owned one of two grocery stores in town and my mother was the postmaster.

During the fall, the population of the town more than doubled as the itinerant workers arrived to pick cotton. On Saturday afternoon, when farmers and workers came to town to buy the week's necessities and whatever small luxuries they could afford, the double lane dirt road that defined the center of town was filled with cars, pick-ups, and an occasional wagon. To get through town, one had to wind his/her way through the randomly parked vehicles.

A community barbecue was the major attraction of Armistice Day. The people of Millersview turned out in full force to honor their veterans and feed themselves and their neighbors. I remember the hand-dug pit about 20 feet long and three feet wide filled with beef, mutton and cabrito. It was located at the back of the school yard. As years went by a permanent pit of similar size was built using cement blocks with a chain link cover to hold the meat. A group of volunteers, mostly veterans, spent all night cooking the meat, drinking a little whiskey and telling stories. Among names I remember are Temple Stevenson, Burton Stevenson, Jack Rainwater, Tom Benge, and Tom Lumbley.

People from outlying parts of the county, who were seldom seen in Millersview, were present at the Armistice Day Celebration. From outside the county there were visitors from Pear Valley, Doole, Salt Gap, Melvin, Eden, Brady, Ballinger, Eola, San Angelo and possibly, Abilene. My judgment as a 10 year old and my memory of 60 years ago is subject to question, but I estimate 1,000 people attended the celebration. A short patriotic program preceded the serving of the barbecue.

Food seemed to materialize from nowhere. Barbecue, beans, potato salad, slaw, and light-bread weighed down the individual plates. Following the meal, the ranchers from around the area put on a goat roping. Small amounts of money changed hands as one favorite went against another. As the afternoon wore on, discussions as to who had the fastest horse, frequently erupted.

It was not unusual to have half-dozen impromptu horse races through town or around the goat roping arena. Friendships were often strained by the outcome of the races.

Sixty years later, I decided to return to the scene of some of my most memorable days. Recently, my sister and I, at the urging of my most enduring friend, Kenneth Barr, drove to Millersview, some 200 miles west/northwest of San Marcos, to the Veteran's Day celebration.

John Deere and paved farm to market roads have made Millersview as obsolete as the mechanical adding machine my grandfather used in his grocery store. It was reported that seventy odd souls, give or take a few, make their home in the vicinity of what was once the bustling, energetic, community.

My expectations were not high. I marveled at the fact that Kenneth invited me to the "November 11th barbecue." How could such a celebration endure in the face of the apathy toward veterans and the major exodus from small town, USA? But the nostalgic urge overcame logic and since my sister, who lives in Wimberley, agreed to go with me, I found myself responding to my old friend's urging.

Already there were 100 people or more gathered at the old school yard. Among them was Fern Schuder who hired me to chop cotton for her when I was 10 years old. She is approaching 90 and is still as energetic as when we were attacking the sour grass and ragweeds along those cotton rows.

The last senior class graduated from Millersview High School in 1958. I'm not sure when the school closed completely, but all the windows are broken, brush and weeds are devouring the building where Nellie Bryson taught me from second through fifth grade. The gymnasium, however, has been preserved as a community building and appears to be as serviceable as it was when it was completed by the WPA in 1939.

At 11:11 AM, all those present stood at attention, hand over heart, as the VFW color guard from San Angelo raised the flag. Immediately following, 15 year old Jessica James, with a remarkably mature soprano voice, rendered The Star Spangled Banner. There were no speeches.

Names of veterans who died in the wars were read. The Greebon brothers, Freddie and Oliver, went down with the Marblehead in the battle of the Coral Sea. Marvin Williams, Jr., and Albert Terasaz, were killed in Korea. There may have been others, but I failed to note them.

A prayer of thanksgiving followed the reading of the names. The "amen" signaled to those present to get in line for the barbecue. A small army of cooks, all male, sliced brisket into serving portions. Women loaded the serving tables with their homemade potato salad, along with beans, sliced onion, pickles, slaw, cakes, pies and bread.

I have no idea how this feast is perpetuated year after year. There were buckets at the head of the lines which subtly suggested one could drop a one, a five, a ten or a twenty, but there were absolutely no prices in sight.

My conversation with the county judge, Allen Amos, revealed there are 3,996 people in Concho County. He hastened to add that number includes the 1,300 inmates, who are all deportable aliens, in the prison at Eden. Over the past 10 years, excluding the prison, he said the population figure has not varied by more than 10 people. Mr. Amos pointed out that Millersview's Veterans' Day celebration is the largest gathering of the year in Concho County.

Concho County encompasses 992 square miles and has two high schools, one at Eden and one at Paint Rock. In football, Eden is a 1A school while Paint Rock plays six-man football.

But size does not determine the heart and spirit of a community. This Veterans' Day, Millersview's population grew from 70 to more than 500. The school grounds were covered with people from Pear Valley, Doole, Salt Gap, Melvin, Eden, Brady, Ballinger, Eola, San Angelo, Abilene, and Millersview, paying homage to the veterans of all wars.

One could almost feel the ghosts of Freddie Greebon, Oliver Greebon, Marvin Williams and Albert Terasaz. My mind went back to Viet Nam and remembered those from Oklahoma, Illinois, Idaho, New Jersey, California, and Wisconsin. They too were honored in this most unlikely way in this most unlikely place. I suspect they will continue to be honored by this hardy group for the next 80 years.
bibb111231@yahoo.com

Cameron's First Day of School

The following was written about five years ago when my daughter prepared her son for his first day of school. With Mother's Day a few days away, it seemed appropriate for young mothers who are often overlooked at this time. I think any mother, regardless of age or era, who has ever packed that first lunch for that first day of school will recognize herself in the few words below.

Cameron is five. He is getting ready to go to a real school for the first time. He is excited about his first day of kindergarten. His mother has prepared him as well as she can for this adventure. She has his uniform and all his school supplies. She has even bought all the food for his first week's lunches. I am not sure who is more anxious about this, Cameron or his mother.

Jamie, Cameron's mother and my daughter, is sorry because she must face the reality that she no longer has a baby, a toddler or an innocent three year old. Cameron's going to school requires her to face the passing of time and admit that nothing stays the same. He is approaching the loss of innocence. He can no longer get away with the behavior of a narcissistic four year old. Fourteen or fifteen other five year olds will insure he learns that lesson. He will stand in line. He will wait his turn. He will sit until he is given permission to rise. And he will be silent until asked to speak.

For five years now, it has largely been him and his mother. Dad entered the picture from time to time, as did big brother, as did grandparents and assorted aunts and uncles, but most of this time, the teachings he has received, his experiences, the landmarks of his life have been initiated and controlled by his mother.

This deep bond between them has provided Cameron with a profound sense of security and safety. He now senses this impending change. This awareness makes him somewhat anxious. He asks questions about being accepted by other kids. He is concerned about his teacher's treatment of him. He seems to know he is moving beyond the reach of his mother's protective wing. It is frightening. But he is good at controlling his anxiety most of the time. The real difficulty is for mom to control her anxiety.

It is important for her to treat this as a part of Cameron's normal passage and not let her fears show through. Cameron is so attuned to her feelings, he will react to her concerns with greater intensity than he will to his own feelings and fears. They have established a communication bond that spans time and distance. It is at an unconscious level and neither is quite aware of its depth and sensitivity.

The emptiness the mother feels is frightening. It makes her aware of the time and effort she has devoted to being a mother and now she will have to share her child with others who will undoubtedly have a profound influence on this innocent creation of hers. But facing reality is a part of the maturing process. We lose those things we love and move on to find other loves or love in different forms. The mother will see how essential others are to Cameron's development. She will come to appreciate their contribution to the finished product.

He will suffer sadness. He will know gladness He will experience the euphoria of success. He will experience the depression of failure. He will see and be a part of miracles. He will have doubts and question the reason for his own existence. He will love. And he will long to be loved.

He is like a sculpture. She has molded a piece of art to be a worthy addition to the world he inhabits. He is to be appreciated by those whose lives he touches. He is to give his environment a new perspective and help others see possibilities instead of obstacles; to see beauty instead of grime; to bring healing instead of pain; to sense the urgency of life instead of the grimness of death.

Other hands will contribute to the final outcome of this child, but she has established the pattern they will build upon. Teachers, coaches, friends, other family members will make contributions, but those contributions will only reinforce, strengthen, enhance and enlarge those elements put there by his mother. The mold is set. He will emerge from the cocoon of childhood to responsibilities of adulthood with patterns of her teachings imbedded in his psyche. He will be her creation.

Locally Owned

"Last locally owned bank won't be for long" read the headline above the story in the San Marcos Daily Record. The story went on to announce that the McCoy family would be selling Balcones Bank to a regional or national financial institution.

Earlier in the week, a letter announcing the liquidation of Steward's Hardware Company arrived in my mailbox.

It is a sign of the times, I suppose, when a faceless corporation or a ubiquitous franchiser, more often than not, controls our businesses. I know there are many businesses in San Marcos that are still locally owned. But it does underline the change occurring in small-town America where, once, all businesses were locally owned.

We have a multitude of locally owned restaurants, clothing stores, garages, and service industries. We are fortunate enough to have three locally owned auto dealerships. However, one must wonder how much longer these businesses can avoid the fate of Balcones Bank and Steward Hardware.

The Outlet Malls and IH 35 have brought a plethora of competition and choices, which is a good thing in most instances. You don't like what you see in *this* store, you can go to *that* store and find it. The big box stores present us with a choice of 27 varieties of denim pants. You can pick up potting soil, golf balls, pharmaceuticals and bacon at one stop. Price is too high in store A. Go across the parking lot to store B.

I suppose I am wallowing in nostalgic inertia when I suggest that I was much more comfortable shopping when I could walk in a store, have the owner or a life-long employee greet me by name and remember what I bought last time I was there. They knew what I needed before I told them.

They knew their business, not just how to sell their wares. That's why I trusted them to give me a proper fit, tell me if I needed new tires, and give me the best deal they could. And, we were friends. I saw them in church, or at the ball game, or Kiwanis meetings.

I grew up in a small town—the zip code is all that remains—where my grandfather owned a grocery store. I remember his "waiting on customers." That meant they told him what they wanted, he took it off the shelves, stacked it on the counter, then rang it up on a mechanical cash register.

He often wrote out a bill and stuck it in his files. No cash changed hands until the cotton was sold in the fall. Not very efficient, but business was done that way.

International Harvester, John Deere and paved farm-to-market roads put him out of business. Maybe for the better.

There is a line in the stage play <u>Inherit the Wind</u> where Henry Drummond, the defense lawyer says: "...Gentlemen, progress has never been a bargain. You've got to pay for it. Sometimes I think there is a man behind the counter who says, 'All right, you can have a telephone, but you will have to give up privacy, the charm of distance.'"

Trying to stem the tide of progress and slow the rate of change in the world is futile. And, of course, we don't really want to. Those who, like me, loudly mourn the loss of innocence and the erosion of community with the onrushing phalanx of Targets and Wal-Marts, gladly glide over four-lane highways in luxury-cushioned and climate controlled automobiles and never make the connection.

Family Lore

My wife and I were married almost 30 years ago. After a year or two of getting together with my family, she pointed out that I, and all my relatives, tell the same stories each time we gather.

She thought they were funny, tolerable or benign the first two or three times she heard them. At first, she laughed out loud. Later, she began to smile politely. Then there was the eye-rolling, and the look on her face that said, "not again." Finally, she just left the room when I or one of my sisters says, "Remember the time..."

Instead of apologizing for it, and attempting to squelch it, I began to realize these stories are family lore. They never change and, for reasons I don't understand, we never tire of telling them. Lore is generally defined as *knowledge possessed by a people or a class, especially when such knowledge is regarded as of a traditional description.* Our lore is nothing if not of a traditional description. We use the same words to describe the same stories time after time. Some of the stories are (or were) funny; some are poignant; some are sad; and I guess some are cruel. But all the stories are important and they help define who we are.

When Aunt Molly was alive, it was impossible for my two sisters and me to gather at her house without her regaling us with the story of her family's journey across west Texas in an ox cart and a covered wagon. She was four. In 1911, it took 18 days to travel from Bronco, on the New Mexico border, to Stacy in Concho County.

Then there is my younger sister, Jane, and the goat. When Jane was about four, one of the local ranchers gave her an orphan kid goat. She fed it with a bottle and naturally, where Jane went the goat was sure to go. One day, she entered the recently constructed WPA outhouse.

The goat came along. As she lifted the lid, the goat's curiosity got the better of him as he leaped upon the stool and went head first, six feet down into several months' accumulation of human waste. Daddy was summoned and, along with a couple other men, fished the goat out of the toilet.

Peanuts was my Shetland pony. When I was about seven or eight, a friend and I were taking turns riding and the saddle slipped, dumping my friend, and sending Peanuts into a frenzied run down the middle of main-street with the saddle suspended under his belly. My mother was the postmaster. From her small window, she only glimpsed horse and saddle. She was certain I had finally committed terminal stupidity and Peanuts was dragging me to death through the middle of town.

A favorite story of mine is about Uncle Mark, mother's brother. He had a penchant for nipping the bourbon a little heavy on occasion. One Saturday afternoon, he was involved in the local poker game and the communal bourbon bottle. When he ran out of money and bourbon, he decided to collect a few debts owed my grandfather. My grandfather owned a local grocery store.

Uncle Mark found a customer who owed a few dollars on his grocery bill. Uncle Mark demanded payment and became belligerent when the customer refused to give him money. To avoid an apparent assault, the customer grabbed an ear of corn from a nearby wagon and threw it and hit Uncle Mark on the lip. It caused profuse bleeding. He was wearing a white shirt. The splattered blood gave him the appearance of Clyde Barrow's last moments. My grandmother spied him when she and my mother came through town from a short trip. Granny asked in a voice of delirium, "Mark, what on earth happened to you?" "Nothing, Momma," he replied. "I just been eatin' roast'n' ears."

There are others which space precludes my sharing. We have come to expect the telling of these stories. They are our family lore, an important ingredient of the glue that holds us together. It gives us a sense of commonality. It is part of our identity.

Family lore allows us to travel back to those wonderfully funny, depressingly sad, and unbelievably cruel moments to recapture the mirth and warmth of the moment; or to attempt to give the sadness a happy outcome; or to right the cruel wrong. It helps us understand who we were and how we became who we are.

The Shadow of Death

How does she die I thought
I've never seen anyone die slowly
Death comes rapidly and erases
A body that is in a space and then is no more
But she's been told and now she knows
Almost exactly the number of her days
And so does she fight the eternal night
That lurks in the recesses of her mind
In ways we have no understanding of
Or does she welcome the end of strife
That fills the life of most of us

Her fight is a valiant one
Her weapons: strength, anger and love
The bones and tubes and machines
Cannot hide the fire in her eyes
The spirit in her voice as she lies
Helpless in the clutches of disease
That has wrenched out her guts and gall
But has not touched a heart that
Reassures us all that she has not been defeated
By this or any other avalanche of tragedy
She fights on to leave us with a legacy of courage

She resides in the depth of our hearts
And reminds us of her love of people
And arts and things funny and crazy
And off center and ordinary
We owe her for her grit and loyalty
And deep sense of right
For the depth of her laugh and
The experiencing of fun
To the bottom of her being
She is and will always be a beacon
Guiding us to our soul

Bibb On
Nina Simpson as she lay dying
In Albuqurque, New Mexico
ca. 1999

Memory of a Friend

As the days go by, the obituaries in various parts of the world contain names once familiar and dear to me. Friends, acquaintances, companions, fellow soldiers, and classmates, are appearing in the obits more and more often.

Recently, another friend's name appeared on that page. He wasn't just a friend. He was that rare person with whom an unbreakable bond was formed in childhood years. That bond was tested by absences, neglect and forgetfulness, but, as we would discover in the last 20 years or so, it never wavered, never weakened and was ever present.

He was a poor kid. His family eked out a bare existence at the subsistence level. Pinto beans and cornbread were the staples at their table. His dad might raise a pig for butchering in late fall, but there were no extras. Their fuel for heating and cooking was mesquite wood gathered from the nearby pasture. Daylight could often be seen through the cracks in the bare and splintered floor of their three room house.

Both of us came from wildly dysfunctional families. In our innocence, we were totally unaware of that fact. And, that label had not been invented. Without boring you with the gory details, suffice to say, our relationship was the most valuable thing either of us owned.

Kenneth Barr and I spent many days in the late 1930s and early 1940s wandering the dry creek beds, the brown pastures, and the dusty fields in the vicinity of the tiny town of Millersview, Texas.

We both learned to swim in the muddy puddles, formed along Mustang Creek when we had rain. In semi-arid Concho County rain was rare. Our birthday suits were our swim suits. Mud squished up between our toes and we were much dirtier when we got out of the water than when we went in.

On the banks of that same creek, we learned to roll and smoke Duke's Mixture tobacco and enjoy the dizzying effect of a deeply inhaled puff. While wandering through the runty mesquite and prickly pear and the algarita berry bushes that survived the dry summers, we scared up jack rabbits, cottontails and an occasional 'possum, skunk or fox. During those rambles, fantastical ideas were formed and excitedly discussed.

We built lean-to's and daydreams on the banks of that mostly dry stream. We built fires and fantasies on the same creek banks. We watched our dogs (mutts, at best) give futile chase to the cottontails and jackrabbits that inhabited the pastures and fields in the area.

Of course, we looked forward to Christmas, but that wasn't the biggest holiday in Millersview. Armistice Day, November 11, was the day we all looked forward to. The population of the town would easily triple. There would be barbecue, goat roping, and maybe a horse race or two and, for sure there would be an over-consumption of alcohol by a number of the inhabitants or visitors and a poker game might erupt into a fist-fight or a similar altercation. Whatever, one could always count on plenty of food and some form of serendipitous entertainment. Kenneth and I hung together, searching for the right fence rail from which to watch the excitement.

As we got older, 10-12 y/o, we were expected to work. World War II wiped the town clean of the able-bodied 18-30 year-olds. Kenneth and I chopped cotton for Jonah King, Moscow Wilson and Mrs. Edwards. We burred (pulled cockleburs by hand from the wool) sheep for Mr. Price, Tom Benge and other ranchers.

In the fall, we played on the cotton bales stored in the gin yard. We climbed to the top of the bales and jumped from one to the other. A mistake in judgment or a leap just short of the target could result in a wallop to the gut that brought an immediate shortness of breath and sharpness of pain. We also wrestled in the burr pit. The gin spit cotton burrs into a pit where they would eventually be burned, but we made them our combat arena before the fires consumed them.

When I was 12, we left Millersview for Abilene. I saw very little of Kenneth for almost 50 years. However, when I made a long-promised trip back, and saw him on one of those memorable Armistice Day (now

Veterans Day) celebrations, it was as if we had just climbed, soaking wet, out of Mustang Creek with a Duke's Mixture in full glow.

His auburn hair almost all gray now; mine, almost all gone. His once rail-like frame filled his ample over-alls; I had an extra 30 pounds, poorly distributed. But, his smile was there. The face of a friend that said, "Nothing's changed."

Our relationship continued for the next 20 years. Infrequent, but deeply experienced trips to Millersview kept our relationship alive and those magical days of a simpler time were re-lived again and again.

Meanwhile, after a stint in the navy and a career as a mail carrier, Kenneth, through his perseverance and frugality, came to own a couple of those farms where we might have worked as children.

A couple years ago, I got word that Kenneth was suffering from a mysterious blood disease and the treatments were more or less experimental. No doctor would predict the likelihood of success. He tolerated the treatments without complaint, maintained the stoic attitude of a Trojan and pressed on.

Then in early September, my sister called from San Angelo informing me that Kenneth had passed away. Along with a throng of 200 or so, I attended his burial. At the ceremony, Kenneth was remembered as a wonderful man. Humble, generous, kind, a great story teller, a lover of the land, a willing worker and a civic stalwart in his community.

Many tears were shed and sorrow was appropriately displayed at the graveside. For me the tears are yet to come. When I remember Kenneth, I can only feel gratitude that I had him as my friend, my crutch, my companion, and a rock on whom I could depend, no matter the circumstances. In him my childhood resided. And he made it bearable.

I can still feel the dry grass under my feet as we ramble through the pastures and laugh at our hapless dogs as they chase that elusive jack rabbit through the mesquite and prickly pear. I can still remember the impractical dreams that got us through the day. I can still feel the closeness of the greatest childhood friend I ever had.

Newspapers

A few nights ago, Brian Williams of *NBC Nightly News* announced that the Manchester Guardian would no longer publish as a daily newspaper. It can be found online, but its days as a print paper are over.

I was saddened. Not because I am a great fan of the Manchester Guardian. I have seen the newspaper no more than a couple of times in my life. I know almost nothing about it. I do remember that, a few years ago, it was often quoted by other publications. A Google search reveals that it is a British publication and is now known as The Guardian. I don't know when "Manchester" was dropped.

What saddens me about the announcement is that I fear the fate of the Guardian is a harbinger of things to come for all newspapers. (Can we call them "newspapers" if they are not printed on paper?)

I suppose there are several factors contributing to this phenomenon. First, is the cost. In the past couple of years we have seen the Austin American-Statesman and the San Marcos Daily Record go to a smaller page format. Most of us would not have noticed had they not announced that it was an economic move. There are other costs. Complicated, expensive machinery associated with printing the paper and delivery of the product to homes and retail outlets are two obvious factors which readily come to mind. Not to mention labor costs associated with all aspects of producing a tangible product. There are probably other expenses of which I am not aware.

The second factor, which I find disheartening, is that young people no longer get their news and information from the newspaper. When I visit my daughter and her family in Houston, I go to the corner convenience store each morning to get a paper. They, like so many in their age bracket, do not subscribe to a daily paper. Coffee and the newspaper are as essential to the beginning of my day as knowing the sun will rise from the east. I'm not sure which is more important to my facing the day, the coffee or the newspaper.

Newspapers have been an important part of my life since I learned to read. In second grade I remember reading the San Angelo Standard Times comics while sprawled on the floor of the tiny post office in Millersview, Texas. I went there after school because my mother was the Postmaster.

Papers have been consolidating or disappearing completely for a number of years. There is no longer a San Antonio Light; The Milwaukee Journal and the Milwaukee Sentinel are now the Milwaukee Journal Sentinel; the hyphen in the Austin American-Statesman masthead indicates that there once was an Austin American and an Austin Statesman; the Houston Post is no longer; the Dallas Times Herald quit publishing a number of years ago.

Given this trend, how long will it be before we get all our news and information from the TV, radio and the internet? Barring some major change in economics and attitude, I suspect that my generation may be the last to care about print newspapers.

Part of my sadness derives from the loss of the unique aspects of newspapers. I just can't imagine myself doing the crossword and the jumble on a computer screen. The comics—one of my favorite sections—just can't be as enjoyable on a computer. I get a certain pleasure from cutting articles out of the paper, putting them in an envelope and sending them by snail mail to family and friends. What will I use to wipe the windows when I can be coaxed into helping with the spring cleaning? While I don't own a bird, what will go in the bottom of bird cages? And, eBay and Craig's List notwithstanding, I have seen nothing on the internet that compares with the value and convenience of the classified section.

Moving from sad to scary is the notion that people will get all their news from the 30 minute newscasts on TV. Much of what we are shown on TV becomes news because it was photographed, not because it is significant. In depth articles and investigative journalism can be found on the internet. However, professional journalism standards are compromised so frequently by bloggers and other alleged news outlets, it is difficult for one to know internet truth from fiction.

Maybe I have reached the stage where I confuse progress with destruction; maybe I'm beginning to believe Milton Wright, a bishop in the United Brethren Church, who said, in the late 19th century, "Everything that is useful has been invented."

Milton Wright was the father of two bicycle mechanics named Wilbur and Orville.

Nostalgia

Nostalgia: *1. The state of being homesick. 2. A wistful or excessively sentimental yearning for return to or of some past period or irrecoverable condition; also something that evokes nostalgia.* Merriam Webster Dictionary online.

My sister's birthday is February 12th and I make a point every year to visit her in San Angelo on or near her birthday. I would like people to think I make the trip because I'm thoughtful, selfless and generous.

Actually, I get more from the trip than anyone. It gives me an opportunity to satisfy that nostalgic urge that, like an irritating itch, will not be satisfied until it is scratched. I usually go alone because my spouse did not grow up in that country (I had to explain to her that we refer to an area of undetermined boundaries as "country") and it holds nothing but boredom for her. She finds the stories we relate ad nauseam even more boring. She has heard them all—more than once.

On the way up, I always stop in Brady and visit Stanley, my high school friend. He lived down the road on the other side of Stingy Lane from Aunt Molly. We rode the same school bus for three years. We spent our summers on a tractor or a combine. We were two of the 13 who graduated from Lohn High School in 1948. Our paths took different turns after high school, and I didn't see him for about 30 years. But when we are together, it is as familiar as if we were meeting in the school hallway, discussing Saturday night's double date.

We discuss people we know, or knew, living and dead; the price of land; the price of cattle; the need for rain; last year's grain crop; last year's cotton crop; the outlook for next year; our health. All this over a plate of the best barbecue within 100 miles. I enjoy it immensely because I can still make Stanley laugh.

I spent the first 12 years of my life in Millersview, about 55 miles east of San Angelo. A few of the buildings that were there when I was a kid are still standing. Only one serves the purpose for which it was built.

The small building that housed the post office that my mother presided over is still there, but it is no longer the post office. The post office resides in a relatively new metal building. And there is a new community center building. Those, along with LeRoy Beech's Millersview Supply store, are the only buildings in use. I'm not sure what LeRoy supplies, but, according to my friend, Kenneth Barr, several people have the keys to the store and if he is closed when they visit the store, they just go in, get what they want and pay him later.

Kenneth lives two miles from the post office, but that is practically in town. He and I have been friends for as long as we can remember. I stop to visit him on my way to San Angelo. We discuss at length those who remain and those who have passed on. He is the best and most enduring friend I have ever had. (He and I pulled all of Granny's green peaches once.) He is closer than a brother to me. Again, we went different ways for a number of years, but when we are together, it feels as if we could be twins. Our stories are repetitious, and to the outsider, must be terribly boring.

My sister and I drove through a lot of the country we traipsed over as kids, remembering people long gone; viewing houses long since silent. Structures once so impressive to a youngster have shrunk significantly. We visited the cemetery where many of our family are memorialized.

In spite of all the obvious changes, I see a sameness that takes me back to my roots and allows me to capture the time that is no more. The Millersview school house, consumed by the weeds and wild mesquite, windows all broken, reverberates with the lessons taught by Nellie Bryson, the memory of Noelene Williams, my first girlfriend, and the playground noises of recess.

I return to these places and immerse myself in the days that were. Ambling along the dry creek beds, and swimming in the muddy stock tanks, and trying out my first BB gun with Kenneth had an influence on who I am today.

The double dates with Stanley, the long, hot, dusty days on the tractor and the combine; basketball practices under Mr. Gassiot; the senior play with Mary Frances—all are part of my DNA.

Visiting those memories scratches that nostalgic itch with which I am afflicted. You should have a similar itch and the opportunity to scratch it from time to time.

Peanuts and the Smart-Aleck

Peanuts was a little bay Shetland gelding, standing no more than 10 or 11 hands. He was a gift to me by my Uncle Mark, my mother's hard-living bachelor brother. I was about seven when Uncle Mark bought Peanuts for me. After about two years of near death experiences and other minor issues with the Peanuts, my dad thought we ought to sell him.

But, first, a little about Peanuts. He was a full-blown equine psychopath, if there is such a thing. Every time I rode him, his poorly hidden agenda was to kill me. He would kick when given the chance. He would grab the bit and run away from time to time, frequently heading directly for a mesquite tree in an effort to scrape me off his back, or smash my head, like an overripe pumpkin against a low-hanging branch.

He was also a horse with Houdini qualities. He would untie a bridle rein or rub the bridle off his head if left tied too long. I frequently found myself on foot, in search of Peanuts. But, he was a horse and I aspired to be a cowboy like Bob Steele, star of the westerns, the staple of the tent-shows which periodically visited Millersview. So, I needed a horse.

However, even I had tired of chasing him all over the country-side and dodging his hooves and teeth. So, selling him was OK with me.

The school superintendent's son, Thomas, was about two years older than I, and he thought of himself as something of a cowboy. He had a habit of razzing me about my escapades with Peanuts, so though we were friends of a sort, there was a distance between us.

I went with Daddy the morning we delivered Peanuts to his new owner. Thomas was eagerly waiting to take ownership of Peanuts.

He sidled up to me and said, "So, he's too much for you to handle, huh?" "Nah, I can ride him," I said, "I'm just tired of him". And there was some truth to that.

"Well, I'll show you how to handle him. I guarantee you I can make him do anything I want him to. You just gotta let 'em know who's boss". Thomas says this with that stupid smirk accenting every word. I didn't cuss at him, but I would have if my daddy and his daddy had not been about five feet away.

Daddy took my old saddle off Peanuts and T. Knox, Thomas' dad, put a new saddle on the pony.

Thomas couldn't wait to climb up on him and show me how to master this little equine murderer who gave me so much trouble. It was salt in my wounds because I was really proud of my riding ability. But something told me to bide my time and hold my tongue. So, when Daddy looked over at Thomas and said, "Well, he's yours Thomas", and Thomas' dad said, "Get on him, son, and show us how to ride him." I just squinted my eyes against the noontime glare of the Texas sun and kept my mouth shut.

Thomas' dad held the reins right at the bit while Thomas mounted. Peanuts stood as still as a statue while Thomas found his seat in the saddle and took up the slack in the reins. T. Knox backed away about two feet and says, "All right take him around the house a couple of times to see how he travels". I swear that little Satan, otherwise known as Peanuts, looked over at me with a mischievous gleam in his eye.

Thomas put his heels into Peanuts's side to move him out. With that, Peanuts blasted off like a roman candle. He shot from his stance in a dead run. Thomas came unbalanced and grabbed for the saddle horn, trying to keep from falling off when, very quickly, it became apparent that falling off might be just the thing to do. Peanuts aimed for a guy wire just beyond the corner of the house. A guy wire is a stabilizing cable, attached at the top of a utility pole and hooked to a 'dead man' in the ground at some angle.

Peanuts went right under the guy wire, but he miscalculated just a bit. I am convinced he simply intended to leave Thomas draped across the guy wire. However, the new saddle caused him to miscalculate the height of the saddle horn and he came just an inch too close to the wire. The wire hit the saddle just below the horn. At the speed Peanuts was traveling, the sudden stop jerked all four of his little feet off the ground at once.

The saddle horn worked like a fulcrum. Peanuts' momentum took him all the way around and over the wire and he landed in a sitting position on the front side of the wire. By some miracle, Thomas escaped injury as he was thrown over the wire, did a complete summersault and landed on his butt, looking back toward where came from. Considerable damage was done to his pride. Otherwise, he was not hurt.

Of course, Daddy and T. Knox sprung into action immediately. Daddy grabbed the pony and T. Knox picked Thomas off the ground and gave him a going over to see if there are any broken bones. "We're gonna' take that little b*****d up to the farm in Talpa", is all T. Knox said.

At that point, I swear that little bay psychopath looked over at me with a grin wide enough to bare his teeth, and seemed to say, "What'd you think of that, Pardner?"

Post Offices

In a recent Austin American-Statesman column, Ken Herman wrote about the imminent closure of some 3,700 small post offices across the country. The Postal Service is several billion dollars in debt, and so cost-cutting is essential. Herman's basic point was that closing some of these offices would be a public relations nightmare for the postal service.

He cited a couple of instances. The post office at Hye, Texas which is located between Stonewall and Johnson City is the facility where Lyndon B. Johnson mailed his first letter at the age of four. Another example of a small post office that is possibly slated for closure is in the Old City neighborhood of Philadelphia. It was established by Benjamin Franklin and is the B. Free Franklin Post Office, so named because that is the way Franklin signed his name. Not only do many of these small post offices have historical significance, there's a blanket of nostalgia covering almost all of them.

There is one of those in my life that takes me back to my childhood like nothing else. Perhaps that's because my mother was the postmaster. (Postmistress sounds so pretentious).

My mother became the postmaster at Millersview, Texas sometime around 1933. I don't remember the event at all and the only way I know the date is because my sister was born, shortly before or shortly after she took the job. That is significant.

The post office was housed in a small building, I'm guessing, about 250 square feet. A wall of individual mail boxes separated my mother's work place from the small room in front where people, mostly farmers and ranchers, gathered each morning to await the arrival of the mail car from Eden. Mr. Ivy drove the mail car. More about him later.

With the arrival of the mail, my mother sorted it and put it "up" in individual boxes. Those who didn't have a box (usually because they couldn't afford the rent) called for their mail at the general delivery window, the single access between the postmaster and the patron. Through this window, she sold stamps, money orders, delivered some mail and carried on the business of the United States Postal Department, then headed by the Postmaster General, a full-fledged cabinet minister.

As mentioned my sister, Jane, or Janie, or Martha Jane, as she was known then, was an infant when mother took the job as postmaster. So, she was taken to the post office every day by my mother, where there was a crib and the necessary amenities to care for a child.

Mr. Ivy, meanwhile, sorted his route mail along with that which was to be delivered to the post office at Paint Rock. He then drove the 14 or so miles along a dusty caliche road to Paint Rock, delivering route mail along the way. At Paint Rock, he dropped off his mail, picked up the Millersview mail and returned.

These memories are of the WWII era, hence gasoline and tires were rationed and not everyone had a car. So, often, Mr. Ivy had a passenger who had business in Paint Rock, the county seat of Concho County.

The post office was much more than a place to pick up the annual Sears, Roebuck catalogue. It was a social center for the exchange of information among the rural folks who populated that parched piece of the Edwards Plateau.

Elbert Whitfield and Bill Bryson, brothers-in-law, talked about the price of cattle. Hiram Price and Frank Evridge exchanged information about the amount of rain received last week. Tom Benge might do a little politicking as he seemed always to be running for county commissioner. Mail was extremely important. It was the connection to an outside world that was far, far away.

In addition to regular mail, Mr. Ivy brought the San Angelo Standard Times to those who subscribed. Headlines contained words like Iwo Jima, Saipan, St. Lo, Paris, Sicily, Arno, and other esoteric places that otherwise would have never crossed the minds of these hard-scrabble farmers and ranchers.

Families such as the Grounds, Greebons, Evridges, Barrs, and Cheathams, were directly affected by those headlines. And, the discussions about the progress of the war occurred in the small room of the post office.

To augment a rather meager income, ranch hands and share-croppers did some trapping in the fall. They brought their furs to the post office to ship to Sears Roebuck. The skunk furs usually retained the all too familiar bouquet we associate with the live specimen. In the spring, everyone in town ordered baby chicks from Sears. Try to imagine 100 little yellow peeps cooped inside a cardboard box for a couple of days. Yes, it smells just the way you imagine it would.

The post office was an essential link to the outside world, as well as the town social center.

Meanwhile, my sister was growing up. As she matured, she became the pet of the town because she was in the post office every day. She was the definition of cute. She had bright red hair, freckles sprinkled all over her face, and an innate ability to charm the horns off a billy goat.

She was a favorite of Mr. Ivy. He brought her chewing gum and a nickel every day. Occasionally, she rode to Paint Rock and back with him. Other post office patrons frequently gave her a nickel or a dime, or some other gift. Once, she received an orphan kid goat from Mr. Hiram Price. That's a subject for another story. Needless to say, I was appropriately jealous of her attention and the largesse it garnered.

Even though the postmaster's job was a civil service position my mother treated it as a sacred public trust. Many nights, as we sat down to supper, there was a tentative knock at the front door. Mother would answer and I would catch the phrase: "Tiene carte para Lopez?" A Mexican farm hand, just finishing a 12 hour day in the fields needed to get his general delivery mail. She always opened the office to deliver that letter.

Millersview still has a post office, albeit, in a new building, but it is on the list to be closed. And, as Mr. Herman suggested, nostalgia will not keep these icons open, but closing them will not erase their subtle contributions to the world they served, nor will the nostalgia associated with them be erased.

Easter 2012

This day was special
And it was you
That made it so

Your love, your caring
And sense of family
Gave it special meaning

There was mutual love;
And respect
And adoration for you

There were expressions
Of feelings
That spoke of love and unity

Your beauty and spirit
Illuminated the day
And renewed all of us

Easter is new beginnings;
You opened your soul
For us to see what can be

This day is imprinted
On my memory in a way
That can not be erased

Bibb for his Friend
4-8-12

Teachers

Teachers have been on my mind a lot lately, I don't know if they are getting more publicity or I'm just growing nostalgic with the season. In the November 28, 2005 issue of Newsweek magazine in Anna Quindlen's *Last Word* column, she begins, *"A couple of years ago I spent the day at an elementary school...I handled three classes and by the time I staggered out the door I wanted to lie down for the rest of the day.... Teaching's the toughest job there is."*

I know many would argue with that. In fact, I have, on occasion, suggested that being a student is the hardest job there is. On the other hand, I reflect on the instructing I did in my military career and it makes me realize that Quindlen is probably right.

I then read in the December 5th Austin American-Statesman about the fourth and eighth graders of Austin schools finishing second in the nation on the National Assessment of Educational Progress exam. The editorial lists several reasons why this happened. It gives credit to the principals, the school board, parents, the superintendent, and yes, to the teachers. But not nearly enough recognition to the teachers.

On December 6th 2005 a front page story of the Austin American-Statesman informs us that the teachers' retirement fund has a $13.2 billion shortfall that will preclude retired teachers receiving an increase in benefits before the end of the decade. It also informs us that retired teachers have not had an increase since 2001. Though inflation has been fairly well contained, that seems a bit unfair when one realizes that over a 10-year period, there is unquestionably a significant rise in the cost of living.

For the past few years, the Texas legislature has wrestled with the problem of funding public education. Their efforts remind one

Crumbs for a Hungry Soul

of a monkey making love to a football. As a result, Texas teachers are among the lowest paid in the nation.

According to Quindlen, "The average new teacher today makes just under $30,000 a year." That is about two-thirds the starting salary of a computer science major, I'm told.

My point in sharing the forgoing information is not to make the point that teachers are overworked and underpaid. That is like saying the sky is blue, it's cold at the North Pole and Nicole Kidman is a hot number. My purpose is to point out the shabby treatment we give to the people who have the greatest influence on the lives of our children.

Some will argue that I'm discounting the parent's influence. That is true in some cases, but when you realize that one out of two marriages end in divorce and that the average parent spends less than a half hour a week face to face with his/her children, I think I have a valid case for the teacher.

This notion started my reflecting on my own teachers and pondering their influence on me.

First, there was Nellie Bryson. She married had a family, and went back to college to get her teaching degree. In my eyes, she was a relatively old teacher—she was older than my mother, which regardless of chronological years made her old. However, it did not seem to affect her energy, and dedication to her kids.

She was my second, third and fourth grade teacher. She never had fewer than two grades in her room. She taught me spelling, long division and something about Texas history. Our history text was an illustrated version—well, it was a pamphlet-sized comic book. I remember vividly, the stories of the Tejas Indians and the story of the Texans, captured after a foray into Mexico, drawing the black beans and the massacre at Goliad.

She also supervised us on the playground, organized our red-rover teams, and kept us from killing ourselves and each other on the swings and merry-go-round.

Day after day, she drilled Bobby Jo Rainwater and me with spelling words until we were able to place first in the County Meet at Eola, Texas.

Next was Vera Faulkner. She taught me English from sophomore to senior at Lohn High School. She was a small bent woman with mousy brown hair in tight curls. Her shoulders were draped in a knit sweater, which emphasized her slouch. Her allergies made her appear sickly, but her gray eyes broadcast enthusiasm, determination and dedication.

She cut through a lame excuse faster than an acetylene torch on butter. She drilled us; she challenged us; we wrote 500 word themes every week; we became friends with Dickens, Shakespeare, Twain, and Hawthorne.

My senior year, she called me to her desk, handed me an application and said, "Fill this out." The issue was not open to discussion.

That application got me into Texas A&M. Vera Faulkner's influence got me out with a bachelor's degree, four years later.

At that same Lohn High School, Clegg Gassiot taught math—all grades, 8-12. He was also the high school principal. And the school superintendent. And the football coach. And the basketball coach. And the baseball/softball coach. And he drove the bus when we played away games. There were no assistants and no secretaries.

When I feel overwhelmed, badly treated, or unappreciated, I think of Clegg Gassiot.

Yes, I know all this was more than 50 years ago. Yes, I know things have changed. I know that a teacher's job has gotten harder and more complex; that teachers put in as many hours today as they did then; that what we *see* in the classroom is the proverbial tip of the iceberg.

But one thing that has not changed is the influence teachers have on our children. Let's hope that our state legislature will get caught up in a fit of conscience and recognize the importance of teachers on our future. Let's hope that when the lege attacks school funding, they will respect today's Nellie Brysons, Vera Faulkners, and Clegg Gassiots.

Eighty

Here I am at eighty and I am never alone
I'm hale and hardy
And enjoying the party
I thought by now I'd be gone

Life itself is a funny thing
It gives and takes away
It's a blessing to be alive today
Because I have had a wonderful fling

If our years are numbered at three score and ten
I'm living on borrowed time
Seems to me I've just reached my prime
At a hundred I'll say "What a ride it's been

Life's been good to me, I'm eager to say
I have known happiness, sorrow and love
With a lot of help from the man above
I can enjoy the good fortune of this day

In life there is always a test
There are good days and bad
There are happy days and sad
And you never know when you are being blessed

11-12-2011

To My Friend

We have lunch
We talk
Two country boys
Of generations past

Common and diverse
We connect
Through trust
And understanding

It's not the years or the tears
Respect and appreciation
Are the glue of
A great Friendship

For my friend, Bob
On his 89th birthday

Trains

WAAAAHOOOOOOOOOOOOOO WAHOOOOOOOOOOO WAHOOOOOOOO!!! That was the first sound I remember hearing when I moved to San Marcos. We came from Killeen to do some work on our newly purchased home on Brown Street. It was a beautiful April night in 1979 so we opened the bedroom windows to enjoy the cool breeze. The house was empty, except for the mattress we had tossed on the floor of the upstairs bedroom.

After a day of cleaning and painting and doing general chores in preparation for our move into the house, we were sufficiently tired to slip into a deep slumber, once our bodies hit the mattress.

We were awakened—nay, we were jolted—out of that peaceful repose by the wail of a train whistle that seemed aimed right at our bedroom. If, as conventional wisdom has it, a tornado sounds like a train, this train sounded like a tornado. After the cobwebs cleared from my brain, I realized I was in no real danger. The train was some distance away, but the sound was loud and assertive on this clear, calm night.

My first thought was, "What have we gotten ourselves into? Is this noise a daily/nightly thing?" I was to find out it is actually an hourly thing.

I have been in San Marcos 32 years. I still live in that house on Brown Street. I now hear that same sound, but instead of sounding like a tornado, it reminds me of the many wonderful train songs that have evoked the sense of adventure, travel, loneliness, pathos, and times past.

Johnny Cash's "Folsom Prison Blues" often crosses my mind when that long freight whistle splits the silence of a calm Texas night:

I hear the train a comin'
It's rollin' 'round the bend
I aint seen the sunshine
Since I don't know when

· · · · · ● ● ● ● ● ● ● ● ● · · · · · ·

Far from Folsom Prison
That's where I want to stay
And, I'd let that lonesome whistle
Blow my Blues away.

Seems to me a shame to silence a sound that can inspire a song such as that. I hate to think that the city is planning to reduce that mournful reminder of our romance with the railroads.

Railroads are part of the romantic past, and if I must say so, present, of this nation. Carl Sandburg's epic poem "Chicago" has the line, *Player with Railroads and the Nation's Freight Handler."* There are so many wonderful songs inspired by trains and their unique sound and place in American lore: Josh Turner's current hit, "Long Black Train;" Willie Nelson's "City of New Orleans;" and Roger Miller's "Engine, Engine Number Nine;" are examples that come to mind along with "Folsom Prison Blues."

I suppose if I lived next to the tracks, I might like to hear fewer and shorter warnings of approaching freights and Amtraks. To my knowledge, there has not been a hue and cry from the San Marcos citizenry to silence the trains. Of course, my knowledge is far from complete when it comes to citizen complaints against the city. There are so many, it is difficult to keep up. Nevertheless, I'm not ready to take serious issue with those who may oppose those frequent WAAAHOOOOOOOOOOOOOOOs.

However, I can't help reflecting on my days in an hierarchical organization and remembering that there was frequently a need to come up with a problem for a solution that had been devised by some bright, eager, intelligent, energetic idiot (see Dilbert in the daily comics of the AA-S).

I am reminded of Spencer Tracy's line as Henry Drummond in "Inherit the Wind:" *Gentlemen, progress has never been a bargain. You have to pay for it. Sometimes I think there's a man who sits behind a desk and says, "Alright, you can have a telephone, but you must lose privacy and the charm of distance...."*

Without those train whistles we are going to lose some of our sense of adventure, travel, loneliness, pathos, and times past. Is it worth it?

Christmas Tree

O Christmas Tree, O Christmas Tree,
How Steadfast are your branches!
Your boughs are green in summer's clime
And through the snows of wintertime
O Christmas Tree, O Christmas Tree
How steadfast are your branches

(The above are English lyrics from the first verse of the German, "O Tannenbaum")

As the Christmas season is about to smack us in the face like a wet dishcloth thrown by a mad housewife, I wince perceptively at the thought of some of the "traditions" that accompany this most holy of Christian holidays. One of the traditions that makes the season, for me, less than a joyous occasion is the Christmas tree.

There are several versions of the history of the Christmas tree, but it is generally agreed that it originated in Germany almost 1,000 years ago. St. Boniface is said to have found pagans worshiping an oak tree. In anger, he cut down the oak tree. A fir tree sprouted in its place. He took this as a sign of the Christian faith. Trees were not brought into the house and decorated until the 16th century. Tree ornaments made their way to England through Queen Victoria, who admired them while visiting her German ancestors.

OK, that is a short—very short—history of the Christmas tree. In my humble opinion, St. Boniface and Queen Victoria did us no favors. Oh, I have a few pleasant memories of Christmas trees, but they escape me at the moment.

Only kidding. When I was a kid, we went to the pasture and cut a small juniper—we called them cedar trees—for Christmas. We decorated it with silvery tinsel, handmade popcorn ropes, looped paper chains and a strand of red and green lights. The tree was small, no more than about three feet tall.

My adult memories of Christmas trees are less than glorious. For example, when we thought we had to have a live tree, one of the chores bound to elicit frayed tempers was selecting a tree. My wife and I would go to the tree lot and my job was to hold the tree erect and her job was to evaluate its symmetry, its fullness, its, color, its size, and its overall suitability to hold the 5,000 lights, 3,000 ornaments and the lighted angel that topped off the tedious effort of applying all those lights and ornaments.

Shopping for a Christmas tree with my tree-decorator took more time than shopping for a daughter's wedding gown. I would pose with every tree on the lot. Too tall; not tall enough; too leggy; branches not thick enough; the left side is no good; the top is no good. You get the picture. I have heard stories of people buying two trees, taking branches from one to fill in bare spaces of the other.

Finally we get home with the tree. Time to attach the tree stand. At this point, it is apparent that this tree has a mind of its own. It leans left. That will never do. It must be straight. Re-attach the tree stand. Now, it leans right. Another iteration of the tree stand. Now it leans forward. After tossing aside all the Christian patience one can muster, cut off half the bottom limbs and stick the thing in a bucket of dirt, and tell the tree-decorator she can compensate for the asymmetry with extra ornaments and lights...or wire it to the wall.

On the rare occasion, one gets the tree to behave in the tree stand, it is important to be prepared for the worst. One year, we had the tree upright and suitably straight, the lights were affixed and the tensil hung piece by tedious piece. A few days before Christmas, we were aroused from our sleep by the horrendous sound of a falling object, mixed with the tinkling of breaking ornaments. This work of beauty, the product of several hours of painstaking effort, had fallen to the floor with a mighty crash.

We righted the tree and the tree-decorator spent most of the next day re-applying the ornaments and tensil in just the perfect places. That night, we heard the same horrendous sound. Sure enough, it was the Christmas tree. The next day, after righting the tree again, I spied the tree-decorator standing about three feet from the tree, tossing tensil in the general direction of the tree. Where it stuck is where it stayed. That which fell to the floor, stayed on the floor. The missing ornaments? Forget it.

We finally got over the live tree habit, especially when they began to cost more than our weekly grocery bill. We also found that fake trees behave better than live ones. That fresh pine scent, so necessary to the festive air of the season, is available in a spray can.

My chore has always been to string the tree lights. I'll not waste a lot of time elaborating on my trying to untangle the mess I put away last year. My tree-decorator is very particular about the lights. Color, placement, depth, and spacing all are subject to her approval. The first effort is just that—a first effort. They are too far out on the limbs; there are too many on the right side; there are not enough toward the bottom. Of course, stringing tree lights would not be complete without having a strand that does not work because of a burned out bulb.

We finally concluded that *steadfast branches* and *boughs of green* vividly represented a case of diminishing returns. Our song is *No Christmas Tree; No Christmas Tree.*

We now visit our daughter at Christmas. She has an eight foot tree, decorated to the fullest. To my knowledge, it has never fallen. I'm almost positive it is wired to the wall.

Prodigal Father, Prodigal Son

He was fourteen
in need
I was ambitious, ambitious
indeed!
And selfish and thoughtless
And determined I knew
what to do
We parted with sad farewell
He looked away as he fought
the thought
This could be the last
He would see of his father
Why bother
His message escaped me completely
The meaning went totally undetected
Rejected

The months were short as weeks
And filled with the nonsense of war;
violence, glory and gore
The message arrived, portending the crisis
Shoplifting and truancy, no way could it be!
Small bother to me
My days were filled with matters of life and death
Boyish pranks and adolescent revolt are no matter
midst artillery clatter
He was screaming forlornly and desperately for me

But his voice was drowned, I couldn't hear
The tour's a year
It was an ordinary day in July
A busy commander and I and the best machine
But fate intervened

Taken from the jungle, my wounds healed
Arriving at home, I found <u>his</u> scar
deeper by far
We need you, the doctor informed
Your son is sick; diagnostic conclusion
Confusion
The Group began, and there I was rebuffed
Intellect and reason, so dependable on face
Totally out of place
Feelings were probed and discoveries were made
Of things repressed and hidden and denied
Occasionally, I lied
But needs unheeded fester and swell
The cloak was pulled from things better left dead
I bled

The insights I found gave me new strength
To pierce the barrier, to destroy the mold
To see his soul
A year and a half, the process was long
It was slow; feelings ascending, descending
Attitudes bending
Feelings and words were emotionally shocking
Finally to admit it was almost a dare
We care

A lifetime ago there was truancy and revolt
There was lethargy and lying and dope
Now, hope
Confusion remains and there are still lots of doubts
Today, he was down, eons ago he would have balked
Instead we talked

Note: Michael, passed in 2010
After working 20 years counseling
adolescent addicts.

Christmas Shopping

'Tis the season to be jolly.'
Not.

Shopping season is here. It was ushered in on Black Friday, the day after Thanksgiving. In Texas, the only thing that approaches the anticipation of that day is the opening day of deer season. I am neither a hunter nor a shopper.

Though I grew up in rural Texas in a farm family whose reverence for the first day of deer season was matched only by a four inch rain in July, I never experienced the apparent euphoria of a 10 point buck at the end of my rifle sights. Likewise, I am not a hunter of merchandise—at bargain prices or otherwise.

San Marcos shoppers are blessed, I suppose. Two outlet malls ("outlet" implies discounts) with 100 modern stores on each side of Center Point Road provide what I have heard described as a shopper's paradise. To paraphrase some unknown wit, "One man's paradise is another man's hell." I must confess; I do not shop. I buy, but I do not shop.

Unlike my former wife and most women I know, I go into a store and, like most men I know, if I find what I'm looking for, I buy it and I'm outa' there. Half-hour is a long shopping trip for me. I have experienced one exception to that rule. When I bought my last bicycle, it took me two weeks to decide to get it. I was not trying to choose between different bicycles; I was trying to rationalize to my inner Scrooge the irrational price of the bicycle.

I'm reasonably sure that the absent Y chromosome in women has been replaced by a shopping chromosome. Women can shop all day without buying anything—sometimes. I have been told that it is important to shop so that one will know when a real bargain appears.

I am also told it is important to know what the latest "big thing" is and where it can be purchased.

I have tried hunting and shopping. I'm no good at either. My former mate gave me a list for the grocery store. I came home with the wrong size, the wrong brand, or the wrong color. On the rare occasion I shop for myself, I get one of three reactions from my former spouse: 1) Do you *really* like that? 2) Is that the *only* one they had? 3) Do you still have the receipt? Actually, I frequently get all three reactions.

I used to think I could buy gifts, but I have since learned that was a myth fostered by my former wife to avoid hurting my feelings. I would buy her a piece of clothing or jewelry I thought she might like and find that it disappeared into the bowels of her closet, never to be seen again. Occasionally, I would see it reappear on my daughter.

Maybe one reason I'm so bad at shopping is that I dislike it so much. My annual trip to the gastroenterologist or my dentist is a welcome respite, compared to a trip to the mall. I was left at home when The Shopper went shopping. She knew I still expected to see 1960 prices and she got tired hearing me say, "Don't you already have one like that?"

Fortunately, I was married to a world class retail therapist. She had an infallible instinct for just the right gift for almost anyone. Further, she knew where to find it and when to get it at just the right price. She observed and listened when people said they would like a particular item. And, remarkably, she remembers their desires or needs at birthday, Christmas or other gift-giving occasions.

So, how does a shopping-impaired individual, such as I, compensate for his utter lack of taste, patience and awareness of the "latest big thing?" I have found one answer that always works. I give portraits of dead presidents or prominent men of history. If you are so inclined to follow my example, I suggest pictures of Presidents Lincoln, Jackson and Grant or prominent men such as Alexander Hamilton and Benjamin Franklin. No one has ever returned one of those gifts.

So, HO! HO! HO! and Merry Christmas to you! While you are shopping, I'll be indulging myself in the intrinsic pleasure of color-coding my sock drawer.

Granny Akers—Peaches

I learned a lot from Granny. She never held herself out as a teacher, but her actions and attitudes were lasting lessons to a young boy. One of the greatest lessons I learned from Granny was forgiveness and compassion. Bear with me.

Millersview, my home town for the first twelve years of my life, was located in Concho County. It is a dry county. And, I don't mean that alcoholic beverages could not be sold. They couldn't, of course. What I mean is, it was a *dry* county. We didn't get much rain. Occasionally, we did and when that happened, it could be a wonderful place.

Food and weather were major concerns to everyone in the county and Granny was no exception. Often, in her case, the former depended greatly on the latter. She grew or raised almost everything she put on her table. The spring and summer were the growing season and that's when there were ample fruits and vegetables for everyone, especially in a good year, i. e, when it rained.

I have vivid memories of Granny and my mother and maybe one or two other women gathering at Granny's house to put up fruits and vegetables. "Canning" was also a term used to describe their activity. They canned assorted vegetables such as green beans, beets, and corn. They also canned fruits such as plums and peaches. Peaches, yea verily, they canned peaches and herein lies the story.

Peaches were the prime canning fruit. Granny had a couple of peach trees from which she would hope to produce enough to eat fresh and have a few to put up for the winter. The product of these trees was almost always supplemented by peaches purchased by Mother and Granny from a peddler from Mason, Stonewall, or Fredericksburg.

They would take an entire day to peel, slice, and process the peaches into peach preserves, "canned peaches," and pickled peaches. Seems to me there would be 30 jars or more of one sort of peach product or another. I occasionally got to help peel. Mother would occasionally take my knife away and send me to play when I took too much peach with the peel.

This process involved a cook stove going full blast in July—no AC, no fans…well, no electricity. But, the end product was worth the sweat and energy required. In fact, the number of quarts of peaches "put up" was a matter of pride among most of the women of the town.

One spring day, when I was about seven, Kenneth, my lifelong friend, and I were meandering through pastures and fields, hoping to jump a jack rabbit to watch our dogs chase him—to this day, my dog has never caught a jack rabbit—when we found ourselves near Granny's house. We were hot and thirsty and Granny's windmill pumped the coldest, sweetest water of any well in town. So, we detoured over to the windmill to slake our thirst. When we had drunk our fill, we started to head toward town when I was distracted by the sight of a young peach tree with limbs drooping almost to the ground. It was loaded with green peaches. I guess we had lots of rain that spring.

Struck by the idea of relieving our boredom and the notion that Granny was always so appreciative of my help, I suggested to Kenneth that we do Granny a big favor and gather all those peaches for her.

Which we proceeded to do.

We took off our shirts and filled each one with green peaches. When we had stripped the tree of peaches, I went to Granny's front door and yelled for her to come see what we had for her. When she saw us, she was speechless. Literally speechless.

As it happened, my mother was at Granny's house. She was furious as only one can be when extremely embarrassed. Perhaps it was short of rage, but not much. She sent Kenneth home immediately. She went to the nearest mesquite tree and broke off a switch. By that time Granny and I were in the yard. When Mother came for me with her switch, Granny stepped between me and her and said in a voice and with an attitude that stopped Mother in her tracks, "Vera! He's just a child!" Momentarily paralyzed, my mother turned. I'm not sure what happened, but she dropped her switch and I believe I saw her hands go to her face and wipe her eyes. bibb111231@yahoo.com

Lessons from Granny–Chickens

Granny Akers taught me lots of things. One of the many things she taught me was that the realities of life and living are filled with irony.

Granny raised almost everything that went on her dining table. She always had a spring garden and a fall garden from which she harvested a variety of vegetables that found their way to her table or the tables of friends and neighbors. In addition to the vegetables, she raised almost all the meat they ate. One of her most common home grown commodities was chicken.

She obtained her peeps in three ways. Early in the spring, maybe as early as February, she ordered baby chicks, usually 100, from Sears and Roebuck. Or she might set eggs in an incubator she kept in the front room of the small house where she and Granddad lived. The third method of obtaining the young peeps was finding a settin' hen. That is, a hen that felt the maternal urge and decided to "nest." Granny would let her nest and in addition to the eggs she might lay on her own, Granny would add a few, so that when the chicks hatched, the hen would have around a dozen baby chicks.

The Sears and Roebuck chicks, along with those that hatched out of the incubator, were put in a small pen with a warming device, called a brooder. They would remain in the brooder pen until they were beginning to feather. The naturally hatched chickens were, of course, the mother hen's responsibility. But, whatever the source, Granny fed and cared for her "brood" with meticulous care, bordering on love.

If there were a heavy rain that might flood the brood pen, she would risk a personal soaking to gather her chicks in a bed sheet and bring them in the house to dry. She had to spread newspapers all over the room to prevent their droppings from staining her floors.

The newspapers did not prevent the stench of the droppings from permeating the house.

She fed those chicks with great regularity and made sure they had water in their trough. If she detected a disease or an infestation, i.e., fleas or mites, she doctored them to health with some of her home remedies. She made sure they had a varmint-proof house in which to roost each night. Fox and skunks were notorious chicken thieves.

One might say she was a human *mother hen.* Those chickens received her devoted and loving attention from their hatching to their demise.

And, I guess their demise is what lends the irony to this memory. After all the loving care, the devotion and the attention, the work and the effort Granny lavished on these fowl, she could gather them all around her by spreading handfuls of grain on the ground and with a stiff wire with a hook at the end, snatch a couple from the flock, and blithely wring their neck until the head separated from the body.

Their ultimate destination was a heaping platter in the center of the dining table.

bibb111231@yahoo.com

Granny Akers—Company

As a result of recent events in my life I have been doing some work to get in touch with my past and the people in it who might have shaped my development and had an influence on my becoming who I am. I have discovered a number of people influenced me in many ways. I have already written about some of them briefly. I have not written about the person who was probably the single greatest influence on my development.

That person is Granny Akers, my maternal grandmother. This piece is retrospective, of course. It is a description of a person seen through the eyes of a child. And if it seems I am ascribing saintly powers to this all too human individual, your perceptions are correct for she was a saint whose 76 years on this earth were a living testimony to all that is good in people.

Granny taught me to accommodate visitors and company and she taught me that company and visitors are what makes solitude so welcome.

One of my most vivid memories of Granny Akers—just Granny to me—was the Sundays my aunts and uncles would come to visit. My family lived nearby, so we didn't travel to Granny's house, but when mother's two sisters and their husbands came to visit, our family naturally gravitated to Granny's house for Sunday dinner.

Sunday dinner usually consisted of fried chicken, cream gravy, mashed potatoes, hot biscuits, and fresh vegetables, i.e., squash, cucumbers, onions, green beans, okra and whatever else might be available from the garden.

Granny always went to the Baptist Church on Sunday. Always. Granddad did not go and that's another story. Back to Sunday dinner.

As I write this, I'm trying to understand how Granny put all this together and went to church, but she did.

The fried chicken had feathers on it when she awoke that Sunday morning. So, she butchered three or four fryers before she left for church at around 11:00 a.m. She had most likely gathered the vegetables beforehand, but she did not cook them until after church. For a Sunday dinner, she would never serve a dish that was not freshly cooked.

The grown up guests were: Aunt Molly and Uncle Bill, Aunt Chuck (Yep, that's right) and Uncle Arliss, mother and daddy, frequently Uncle Mark, and, if the itinerant Baptist preacher came to Millersview that Sunday, he would be present. Add Granny and Granddad and that's 10 people. In addition, there were three of us grandkids—later there would be a fourth.

The grandkids ate at a separate table or a second table. That's how I learned to like chicken livers, gizzards, backs, racks and wings. That's what was left for the kids.

Granny prepared this meal for roughly 13 people on a wood cook stove initially. As progress crept into west Texas, she eventually got a kerosene cook stove.

Of course the girls helped Granny get all this to the table. The men sat on the front porch, smoked, talked about the dry weather, the price of lambs and what the cotton crop looked like.

After dinner, the girls helped Granny do the dishes, put away leftovers and clean the kitchen. The men sat on the front porch, smoked, talked about the dry weather, the price of lambs and what the cotton crop looked like.

Around 4:00 o'clock, Aunt Molly and Uncle Bill, Aunt Chuck and Uncle Arliss, and Uncle Mark would leave for their respective homes. Mother and Daddy would say their goodbyes and go home. If I were lucky, Mother would let me spend the night with Granny.

One evening, after a typical Sunday dinner, just at dusk, Granny and I were sitting in the swing on the front porch. She let out a big sigh and turned to me and said, "Sonny Boy, I just love having everybody here at the house, but it is so lonesome when they leave." After a brief pause, she turned to me again and along with an even deeper sigh, she muttered, almost under her breath, "But it's a good lonesome."

Tolerance

On the eve of Martin Luther King's birthday, it seems appropriate to consider the true meaning of tolerance and its effect on our nation. In a nation founded on the principles of acceptance, opportunity, equality, and fundamental rights such as suffrage, free speech, freedom of worship, freedom of the press, and rule of law, it is mind boggling to look back and recognize the oppression suffered by generations because of intolerance.

Tolerance is more than not discriminating. It is more than accepting. It is more than 'having black friends.' It is recognizing and lauding differences. It is learning new ways of dealing with old problems. It is discovering all one can about that which is different. We have made great strides in this direction, but today our schools, the laboratory where the great social experiment of racial integration can be most easily observed, are still dealing with issues of understanding. Courses in black history, cultural celebrations, recognition of historic dates, such as Cinco de Mayo are often resented. Sometimes openly, sometimes subtly.

Those of us over the age of 40 have been taught or, at least have experienced stereotyping in our lifetime. You will recognize the innocuous—to many of us—expression, "All Asians look alike." The second, "truth" we knew about Asians was that they did not value life as deeply as we did. The "N word" was ubiquitous. It was a common part of our language. Hispanics were commonly referred to by derogatory names and their language was derided because it was strange to those of us who did not understand it.

The mystery, it seems, is not with the fact that the African-American, the Hispanic, the Asian and the Native American have the temerity to demand what is rightfully theirs. The mystery is that we have not had a revolution in which they sought to right the many wrongs perpetrated in this country in the name of progress, economics, or even equality.

Tolerance is a civilizing influence. Intolerance thrives on ignorance, and promotes fear, anxiety and segregation. Tolerance moves us from the child to the adult; from lashing out to willingly enfolding; from exclusion to inclusion; from demand to compromise. Tolerance promotes cooperation and reduces self-involvement and helps our aims to find a common target. Tolerance is the bridge that gets us from hate to love; from exclusion to acceptance; from ignorance to understanding. Tolerance is the oil that smoothes and enhances the path to peace.

If one must be taught to hate, as Rogers and Hammerstein explained in <u>South Pacific,</u> one of the most popular musicals ever performed, one must be taught ways to hate. One of the ways we are taught is to dehumanize. Our military, in combat, adopts an effective means of dehumanization. We assign derisive names to people whom we would find to be good friends under other circumstances. Remember the Huns; the Japs; the Slopes; the Chinks; the Krauts; the Slant-eyes? That makes them different than we are. Consequently, they are less than human.

In the military, this practice serves a purpose. It is not so difficult to take the life of a dehumanized Homo Sapiens, as it is to kill a person, if you reflect that the person might have a wife, husband, child, mother, father.

So, when will we arrive at the point that "tolerance" is no longer necessary? We will simply understand the truth of Jefferson's... "all men are created equal."

Things I Didn't Do

Sometimes your life can be defined by the things you did not do. When I was a therapist, I told my clients that you are often defined by the things to which you say no. In short, we need to establish boundaries, outside which we decide not to go and inside which, we do not allow others to trespass. These boundaries are important because they help us maintain stability and consistency and help others to know who we are.

I been thinkin' about things I'm glad I didn't do. First among those things is I'm glad I didn't invest in emus or ostriches when $30,000.00 was a good price for a breeding pair. Remember when people with the notion of immediate riches were lining up to buy those big birds. Ostrich meat was going to replace beef as the lean cuisine of the future. Emu oil would cure everything from arthritis to zits. People, I seem to recall, were actually buying the right to the eggs. That is, they were purchasing emu and ostrich futures.

I'm glad I didn't move to San Antonio when I retired. My wife I were on our way from Killeen to San Antonio to peruse the real estate in that city when we decided to stop in San Marcos for a cup of coffee. While sitting in Sambo's (long since gone), she picked up a copy of the Daily Record, called a real estate agent and we left town that evening with a contract on our house. I had not planned to retire for two to three years. We were settled in San Marcos in three months.

I'm glad I didn't buy a pet rock in the 80's. It isn't that I'm not an easy mark. I most assuredly am. But even I could not be suckered into that idiocy. I have to give someone credit. The brilliance of that scam lay in its simplicity. I have a notion some business or psychology professor assigned one of the slow members of his/her class to come up with an experiment to determine the level of gullibility of the American public. The student did not know the meaning of gullibility and when he asked one of his classmates what it meant the classmate replied, "If you were drop dead, stone cold, dyed in the wool, hopelessly lost gullible, you would buy a rock and call it a pet." And that's how the Pet Rock thing got started.

I'm glad I didn't talk myself out of buying a bicycle. There are a dozen reasons why I should not own a bicycle. There are too many hills in the San Marcos area. There are too many cars on the streets. It is too dangerous. I am too old. That little hat looks ridiculous. You have no one to ride with. OK, if you are going to be picky, there are a half-dozen reasons why I should not own a bicycle.

I'm glad I didn't buy a time-share condo when that was all the rage. I have met lots of folks who were talked into that legal scam. They: 1) Don't use the time they bought and find it almost impossible to sell or give away; 2) Have been assessed a sizable maintenance fee for services or repairs after the fact; 3) No longer are able to go to Ruidoso, Corpus Christi, Galveston, Santa Fe or wherever their condo is located; 4) Find the time allotted to them is right in the middle of their busiest season of the year.

I'm glad I did not smoke pot, drop acid or shoot up with even more powerful stuff. For my generation, the drugs of choice were alcohol and tobacco. I over indulged with both of those, but never lost the ability to control my day to day behavior and never became debilitated by either. Part of my luck lies in the innocence of the era of my youth. I am most assuredly no wiser, nor am I more saintly than later generations. I was not presented the same opportunities for self-destruction they were.

Don't ask about all the things I did that I wish I had not done. That is a much longer list and is the subject for another column. Paring it down will be a major task. Meanwhile, thank whatever circumstance it was that helped you elude a few of the stupid opportunities that have come your way. If you would like to share a few of those 'missed' opportunities, drop a line to the editor or send me an email.

The Electronic Age

I have had a computer since 1986. My first one was a Commodore 64, I think. It had no hard drive. When I decided to upgrade, I purchased a 20 kilobyte hard drive, and my neighbor installed it. I don't even remember what the thing was capable of, but you can assume it was very little. I do remember that the Commodore cost me $1100.00... without the hard drive.

I have had two desk tops and a lap top since that initial foray into the nether world of the electronic wonderland. From that introduction, one might think I am some sort of electronics geek. That would be wrong. Since 1986, I have learned almost nothing about electronics. It is still science fiction to me.

While a veritable flood of electronic gadgets has appeared on the market since that time, I have avoided as many as possible.

Since the early 90's, the "latest big thing" has changed about every six months. There was the car phone, perhaps the first mobile phone. It plugged into the cigarette lighter outlet. It was roughly the size of a bread box and weighed about eight pounds. The receiver/transmitter was similar to that of a conventional phone. My wife convinced me we needed one for emergencies because at the time she was frequently driving to Houston to baby-sit for our daughter who was a flight attendant. If you have ever driven IH-10 to Houston and IH-45 through Houston, you would have to agree with her.

I never really learned to use the thing in spite of its simplicity. Also, I seldom heard it ring, so for me, it was a nuisance.

Then the deluge began. Laptops appeared. No longer was computer use limited by the presence of an electric/phone outlet. Every time I boarded an airplane, which wasn't often, it seemed every passenger except me was engrossed in whatever was on his/her lap top. Nobody spoke to anyone because his/her attention was focused on the little screen.

That changed. As computer technology advanced, so did telephone technology. Instead of no one talking, everyone began talking... to their cell phones. If one were in a waiting area, a restaurant, or walking down the street, one might suddenly hear one side of an animated conversation. Look around to see if someone is trying to get your attention and then, embarrassed, you realize they are on a phone talking to goodness knows whom.

In the land of electronics, smaller is better, so it wasn't long before the Palm Pilot made its appearance and replaced the lap top as a travel companion. Never could figure out what that thing did. Still don't know.

Smaller phones followed. The car phone became a Neanderthal that embarrassed my wife when she had anyone other than me in the car with her. So, we replaced it with the cell phone. At this point, I have to admit, our cell phones, though small, are horse and buggy, comparatively speaking. They do not do photographs; they do not record music; they do not receive television transmissions; and they do not prepare meals.

We can talk to each other. And the amazing thing about that is that when she is in North Carolina, it is a local call when she calls me in San Marcos. "What a cooouuntry," as the Russian comedian, Yakov Smirnoff, used to say.

When people stood in line for 24 hours outside Best Buy to get an I-phone, I had no idea what was happening.

Television ushered electronics into the home. Those who are over 60 will remember black and white TV. Younger folks have always had color. Likewise, younger people have always had a VCR or a DVD. Yes, we have one of each. And no, I can't operate either.

If I am asked to record "Gray's Anatomy" or "Dancing with the Stars," someone has to be on the cell phone (I can take it to the TV) and guide me through the steps required to program the recorder.

I suppose if it were up to me to operate the VCR, it would still be incessantly blinking 12:00. My grandson stayed with me when his mother and grandmother went on shopping trips. He would bring his favorite movies—I have seen "Miss Congeniality" 64 times—for the VCR. He had to set up the TV and program the VCR. He was seven years old at the time.

While, I have no delusions about keeping up with the younger generations, nor do I want to go back to writing on an Underwood (no relation) typewriter, I glance up from my keyboard and catch sight of a well preserved wooden tennis racket, and experience a wave of nostalgia.

Note to self: Get cycling partner to program cell phone number in my cell phone.

Anna Nicole Smith

Have you had your fill of Vickie Hogan? She has been front page news in the Austin American-Statesman; she has been wall to wall on television, especially the cable news channels; and she has had a lot more coverage than she deserves in the weekly news magazines. By the time you read this, I expect most of the frenzy will have abated and we will be swamped with dire reports of blizzards in Chicago (what else would you expect this time of year?) or Paris Hilton will have decided to get another dog.

What, you've never heard of Vickie Hogan? Well, that was her name before she took off her clothes for *Playboy*. Somewhere along the way, she managed to marry an eighty-four year old multi-millionaire who conveniently passed away not long afterward. She is better known to all of us today as Anna Nicole Smith. She once had a reality show which was anything but real. Mostly, she appeared fashion-challenged, zonked out on drugs, slurring her words and showing off the extraordinarily tacky furnishings of her mansion.

Would someone please explain to me our sick obsession with the death of this poor soul? Clearly, the death of anyone is, at least, a sad and regrettable occasion. It may be a tragedy for a select group of people. But the death of most of us will pass unnoticed, and unheralded by all but a miniscule percentage of the population.

For example, the recent passing of James Brown, the Godfather of Soul, a renowned musician, whose genius changed the world of pop music, barely received more than a couple of days of cable news coverage. In fact, his funeral may have lasted longer than the news channels' preoccupation with his death.

How does Anna Nicole's death create such a feeding frenzy among the media? Pictures of her in every conceivable situation are looped endlessly as some talking head reads five minutes worth of drivel about her or her five-month old child. Who might the father be? Who is the latest money-grubbing, publicity-seeking slime-bag to crawl out of his rat-hole and claim paternity? Did she overdose on drugs—prescription or otherwise? And, the real bombshell of breaking news, why did she have Slimfast in her refrigerator when she was a spokesperson for TrimSpa?

Granted, Anna Nicole was famous. But for what? Being famous? When Judge Judy Sheindlin was asked about Anna Nicole, her reaction was similar to my own. Has she written a book, has she painted a picture, can she sing, what has she contributed?

Of course, she is not the first vapid personality to become fodder for the 24/7 news cycles. Remember a few months ago when the disappearance of teen-ager Natalee Holloway was the topic of every talking-head on cable? OK, she was in the prime of life, a beautiful blonde, disappeared under questionable circumstances and there was the appearance of a cover-up. However, I could not help asking myself, during those months of frenzied coverage, how many other young women disappeared under similar circumstances in the same time frame? Or worse, how many soldiers of similar age, died in Iraq. Where were their individual stories, with the cameras lingering on grieving parents, wives or children?

There is a trial of major importance underway in Washington, D.C., the outcome of which could reveal major malfeasance at the highest level of government. It could reveal, whether and how international intelligence was manipulated to take us to war. How many stories of that trial have you seen on your regular news shows or cable news? How many of you, dear readers, can name the principal actor in said trial?

By the way, have they found out why Anna Nicole had Slimfast in her refrigerator?

Predictions 2007

I note that Pat Robertson has been speaking to God again and God told him there would be a catastrophe in the United States this year—2007—that would kill millions of Americans. He could not say for sure that it would be a nuclear disaster, but I understand it would be something like that.

Well, God has not been speaking to me again. He has not told me anything about the coming year. Nevertheless, my prescient vision tells me of many important events that will occur during the next 12 months. I'm sure you will be most interested to learn about them.

The only real catastrophe I can foresee in the near future is that the Texas Legislature will convene on January 9th. No one who is not on strong medication and under the care of a physician would hazard a guess about the havoc this body may bring to the great state of Texas.

However, a few things we might want to be alert for include:

- After 17 days of heated debate and one fist-fight on the floor, the House will pass a bill making the prickly pear the official cactus of Texas.
- Jeff Wentworth will introduce a bill giving the San Antonio River Authority sole rights to all the water in the Edwards Aquifer.
- After the regular session, the Governor will call a special session to resolve the burning issue of what to do about the

Confederate statues on the Austin campus of the University of Texas.

• Budgets for all social services will be slashed, and the federal government will withhold millions of dollars in matching funds.

Since toll roads are gaining momentum in the state, Martindale will construct a toll booth at the intersection of Highway 80 and County Road 142. The toll fees will allow the city to collect sufficient funds to offset the income generated by the traffic Nazi who patrols Highway 80. Along the same lines, Hunter Road will be widened to four lanes from San Marcos to Gruene and will become a toll road. Ranch Road 12 to Wimberley will get the same treatment.

The city council will approve millions of dollars in incentive funds for a descendent of P.T. (There's a sucker born every minute) Barnum to come to town and build an amusement park It will be adjacent to the hotel, constructed by John Q. Hammons.

The recently completed Wonder World overpass will be closed for three months, beginning June 1st, for widening or for repairs.

Five new bars will open on the square. Twelve new restaurants will open and 13 will close.

Enrollment at Texas State will exceed 30,000. The upside of that is that Palmers, Mamacitas, Chilis, Johnny Carinos, et al will have affordable labor. However, each student will obtain two dogs and a cat which they will leave behind when they return home or graduate, and each student will own 1.5 cars.

Apartment complexes with names like Pine Tree Village and Lone Oak Terrace will replace cornfields between I-35 and Martindale.

The connector between Wonder World Drive and Ranch Road 12 will be postponed for another three years. Funds for the road will be diverted to the amusement park mentioned above.

The new school superintendent, whoever he may be, will immediately pronounce the new high school overcrowded and call for a new bond package.

Kyle will pass San Marcos in population and demand that it become the county seat because it is more centrally located. Wimberley will call a special election to un-incorporate. A Wimberley faction will attempt to block the widening of Ranch Road 12.

Since Joe Jamail and Red McCombs have glutted the coffers of the University of Texas, John O'Quinn will give $10 million to Texas State for a new law school. And you thought Jerry Supple was a great fund raiser.

Austin Community College will not conduct a petition drive to convince San Marcos to fund a new campus.

Lance Armstrong will enter the San Marcos River Water Safari. (Only kidding, but if he did, he would lose to Texas State's Erin McGee in the solo kayak category.)

City Council will give lip-service to hike and bike trail construction, but funds for the trails will be diverted to the amusement park incentives mentioned above.

As with any prognosticator, I don't want to be held accountable for every prediction I make. If I get 70 percent, that will be twice as good as Joe Mauer (AL) and Freddy Sanchez (NL), batting champions of their respective leagues this year. Of course, I know that is comparing apples to oranges, but it seems to work for everyone else.

Predictions—2013

Almost every columnist makes predictions at the beginning of each New Year. Those that have a bit of common sense refrain from such a frustrating, futile and facile endeavor. Most of the really good, thoughtful columnists use their space for more important and less inane pursuits. Since I have never been accused of being really good, nor thoughtful, brace yourself for an early dose of inanity in 2013.

1. The Texas Lege, as Molly Ivins labeled it, convened on January 8, this year. They will enact legislation mandating all teachers be armed with a pistol with a laser sight, capable of killing a coyote at 20 paces.

2. Rick Perry will lobby the lege to make him governor for life. Or, has that already been done?

3. Mack Brown, coach of the Longhorns, will receive a $250,000.00 a year raise, making his salary roughly equal to the GDP of Kazakhstan.

4. State Senator, Dan Patrick, chairman of the lege's Education Committee will introduce a bill requiring all teachers be tested every six months on the Old Testament.

5. Texas State University will purchase the north side of the courthouse square and erect a 500 unit apartment complex with underground parking to partially accommodate the anticipated enrollment of 50,000 students in 2014.

6. Unfortunately, the move of the Bobcat football program to the Sun Belt Conference will not be very sunny.

7. The Texas Aggies will win the Southeast Conference by beating Tennessee for the title. They will then beat the Southern Mississippi Golden Eagles for the national championship. (I told you, I'm a pathological optimist. I also assume that only a few of my readers follow Southeast Conference football.)

8. Johnny Manziel will win the Heisman Trophy for the second year in a row. (See items 6 & 7 above.)

9. Ranch Road 12 will be widened to four lanes from San Marcos to Wimberley and will become a toll road. Hunter Road from San Marcos to Gruene will enjoy (suffer?) the same fate.

10. Three people will be arrested for violating the new park rules on alcoholic beverages. None will be prosecuted. City Council will promote these statistics as proof that the rules are working.

11. The Hays County Commissioners' Court will declare the new Hays County office building, commonly known as the Taj Mahal, too small to accommodate the growing needs of the county and will select a site in Kyle for the location of the new building.

12. Kyle will agitate to become the county seat of Hays County, since its population will surpass that of San Marcos and it is more centrally located in the county.

13. Barrack Obama will put on his LBJ pants and twist enough arms and shame enough congress members to pass immigration reform. Whereupon, Governor Perry will announce that Texas will, once again, secede from the Union.

That's my baker's dozen crazy predictions for 2013. They have no scientific basis. To many, they probably have no basis at all. As a prognosticator, I will confess that I predicted the correct outcome of fewer than half the 35 football bowl games played this year.

On the topic of scientific selection, it is interesting to note that I belonged to a pool of 10 or 12 people who attempted to divine the winners of said bowl games. The winner of the pool selected her favorites based on the school with the shortest name. So much for science.

In spite of the tongue-in-cheek nature of my gander into the future, I would remind the reader that I wrote a similar column in 2007 in which I predicted that enrollment at Texas State would exceed 30,000. I guess you could accuse me of picking the low-hanging fruit in that case. I also predicted that the Wonder World Drive extension to Ranch Road 12 would be postponed for another three years and that was just about on the money.

In 2007, I said the new SMCISD superintendent would call for a bond issue to build a new high school. Have you driven out McCarty Lane recently?

Another of my 2007 predictions was that the budgets for all social services will be slashed by the legislature and the federal government will withhold millions of dollars in matching funds.

Maybe the single most important aspect to prognostication is to employ the old adage, "The more things change, the more they stay the same."

Ever the optimist, for you, dear reader, I predict good fortune, good health and good news.

A Stab in the Back

It was about August 1st of this year (2010). I was spending a month in Keystone, Colorado and enjoying the hiking and biking trails in that area. It was a clear cool day, perfect for a bike ride. I decided to head for Copper Mountain, with the notion of continuing on up to Vail Pass if I felt the urge. At the coffee stop at Copper, I became engaged in a conversation with a group of geezers about my own age and time got away from me, so I cancelled plans for Vail Pass.

When I returned to Keystone, I had ridden about 40 miles and thought that was pretty good for my present level of conditioning. I began to look forward to riding up Ute Pass and Montezuma in the near future.

Next morning, when I rolled out of bed, there was a painful knot in the lower regions of my back and with every step I took, it squeezed tighter and more painfully. The pain ran down my back to my hamstrings. Walking was excruciating. Standing was only slightly less so. As the day wore on, I discovered several aspirin made it possible to walk to the convenience store across the street for a newspaper.

My expert diagnosis (I'm not a doctor and I don't even play one on TV) was that I had strained a muscle or two and the pain would disappear in a few days. A few days of pampering went by and the only relief came from the aspirin. Maybe this isn't a muscle strain after all. I decided to leave Colorado early in order to see my San Marcos doctor.

A doctor visit, x-rays, MRIs, a referral and sure enough, it wasn't a muscle strain. It was spinal stenosis which is a scientific term for narrowing of the spinal column so that it squeezes the spinal cord. Beyond that, I'm lost.

OK, we'll get 'er fixed and I'll be back on my bike in a few weeks. That referral I mentioned in the forgoing paragraph brought a simple reflex test, which indicated that while I had a problem in my lower back, there was a more serious problem in the cervical (neck) region. Surgery was recommended, and soon. Well...as soon as I had a myelogram, a stress test, and an echocardiogram. All those took time. Seems some of those tests were necessary to insure that, at my advanced age I could withstand the surgery. (Didn't I tell you that all this began after a 40 mile bike ride?)

October 5th, I was wheeled into the control room of the NASA Space Center—actually, it was the operating room at St. David's Hospital in Austin. There were so many needles, tubes, electrodes, and other connections hooked to me, I could have passed for Dr. Frankenstein's monster. There were so many people in surgical gowns, caps and masks, I thought I was an exhibit for an AMA convention.

The next thing I know, I'm in a hospital room, still hooked up to who knows what, but I can recognize my friend, my sister, and a couple of other folks. They are not wearing masks and surgical gowns. However, their countenance is rather vague, as are the rest of my surroundings. I'm told I did well and the surgery was successful. I have no idea what I did, but I suppose I did it well.

Then the parade began. The surgeon comes in and, sort of like a football coach, gives me a thumbs up and congratulates me on how "well we did." (I think that means I didn't die on the operating table.) Then a nurse comes in and takes my pulse, blood pressure, and whatever else is included in "vital signs." She asks if I need to use the bathroom. An hour later, a physical therapist comes in and takes my blood pressure, pulse and whatever else is included in "vital signs." She asks if I need to use the bathroom. Not long after, the night nurse comes in and takes my blood pressure, pulse and whatever else is included in "vital signs." He asks if I need to use the bathroom. There were others, I think, but you get the picture.

All this occurred on a Wednesday. I spent Wednesday and Thursday nights in the hospital and then they unhooked me from all the needles, probes, tubes, and monitors and sent me home with an eight-inch scar from the nape of my neck to the middle of my back along with a plastic and foam rubber collar the size of a small inner tube. There was a time when mules wore the same size collar.

When I got home, I thought I was fully recovered, but there are witnesses who tell me differently. I understand my mood was hardly that of the cool, mellow gentleman I imagine myself to be most of the time. Further, I'm told that my memory of events was somewhat askew. And, much to my dismay, my physical abilities and balance were hardly up to normal.

After about four days of putting up with psychotic moods, frequent middle of the night awakenings and other little inconveniences of caring for a temperamental 79 y/o who regressed to a temperamental two y/o, my sister went home and I was left to care for myself. I think she needed a recuperation period worse than I.

With the help of a home health agency that provided a visiting nurse, a physical therapist and certain mobility and sanitation aids, I am once again my normal cool, mellow, gentlemanly self. I walk about 3.5 miles a day to stay limber, manage to get most of my meals without help, go to church on Sunday and take in an occasional movie or go out to dinner. I'm still not driving, so I feel a little like I'm on house arrest. But, that's not too bad. I sort of milk that to get my friend to visit me more than she otherwise might.

Ode to an Old Friend—Wiley Phillips

It was the fall of 1948
We passed through the annex gate
A teen-ager fresh out of high school
An eager, but scared young fool

We learned a new language the first few days
Fish, Howdy, Pisshead, and other new ways
To conduct our life in keeping with tradition
And save our ass from holy perdition

The following year we lived in dorm ten
With a cap down on our nose, we thought we were men
As *Pissheads*, we were the meanest of all
Until we met a *Sergebutt* coming down the hall

In 1950, we moved to dorm one
This would be the year we could have some fun
There were dates, Corps Trips and lots of booze
The team was often outscored, but it never did lose

As Seniors, we were the campus elite
Boots and spurs adorned our feet
Only a third of those who passed through the Annex gate
Would attend the ring dance and graduate

But there you were, one of the blessed
With Martha's help, you had passed the test
Out into the world, you went
Never imagining you might experience this honored event

So here you sit at seventy years
I expect the laughter far outweighs the tears
You have served your country, your family and your school
A great man was created from that eager young fool

None of us knows what the future may hold
So, at the risk of using a phrase somewhat trite and old
We just came here to say
We wish you a HAAPPPYYY 70th BIRTHDAY

Bibb9-27-2001

Technology

Confession: I am a techno-illiterate. I do not have a flat-screen TV. I do not have an I-Pad. I do not understand the I-Pod. I have no I-Tunes on my telephone. I do not do Facebook. I do not Twitter. You-tube and blogging are mysteries to me. I can use my I-Phone to make a call, text and take a picture.

OK, so I'm way behind the times. Truth be known, I'm quite happy being way behind the times. I am typing this piece on my computer. So, I'm ahead of my brother-in-law who has no computer. Of course, the only tasks I do on this computer are: writing, i.e., letters and articles such as this one; email; and I am addicted to Free Cell.

Recently, I was at the house of friends and they asked if I watched a certain TV show. When I replied in the negative, they insisted I should see a couple of episodes. Whereupon, they activated their flat-screen TV which covers about half the wall in their den, hit a few buttons on a remote control gadget that I'm sure would control the Mars Rover if they were so inclined. Moments later, there was upon the TV screen an episode of the particular show my friends wanted me to see. Of course, it had aired last week, but by some miracle of technology, they were able to access the thing as if they were pulling a book off the shelf.

A total mystery to me. How do they do that? I am reminded of a story of three men discussing the world's greatest invention. One suggested the automobile. Another suggested the airplane. The third man, studied a moment and blurted, "the thermos bottle." The other two, astonished, asked, why the thermos bottle? "Well," the third man replied, "it keeps cold stuff cold and hot stuff hot. How does it know?"

About a year ago, my daughter who lives in another city, was in a minor panic because I did not have a phone with which I could send and receive text messages. So, to assuage her concern, I took myself straight-away to a vendor of said phones. Whereupon, they *gave* me a phone for signing a contract that gives their corporate parent the rights to all my communications from now to eternity. That includes any messages I might send from the grave. Well…who's to know? Technology, sheesh!

Of course, I pay dearly for the privilege of using this small device. On the other hand, I can call Thailand at no extra cost.

This little device fits snugly into a pocket and has become an essential part of my daily wardrobe. I would no more think of leaving the house without my phone, than I would go out without my wallet. How quickly and how easily we are trained to be the servants of the latest "big thing."

That raises the question of etiquette where technology is concerned. We have all been the victim of a loud, one-sided conversation while attempting to have a quiet meal and a private conversation in a restaurant. Sometimes it happens while we are sitting in the doctor's office, reading last year's Texas Monthly. I know you have been in the movie when the Beatles, *Hey Jude* ring tone goes off.

Another question. Will the mobile phone make the telephone directory obsolete? I certainly hope not. How will I find all the addresses I need? What's my plumber's number? Who does home repairs and how do I contact them? And I don't have all the restaurants in town on my contact list.

Technology has its pitfalls even emails, the ubiquitous and seemingly innocuous means by which we so frequently communicate with our fellow computer users. If you have doubts about that, ask a couple of seemingly straight-arrow generals who were forced to leave extremely prestigious and responsible jobs as a result of expressing some very private thoughts via emails.

Apparently, if you put it on the internet, you might as well publish it in the New York Times. I understand—not sure about this—that whatever goes on a computer is like nuclear waste. It lasts forever. And, like nuclear waste can cause great damage if not properly handled.

I'm sure there are many technological advances in store for us. I'm also just as sure that I will never be able to keep up with them. As a matter of fact, I have exhausted what I have to say about technology.

Now, if I can just get this article attached to an email and sent to the San Marcos Daily Record, I will have extended my technological savvy to its ultimate extent. If you are reading this, you know I am smiling contentedly as I take great satisfaction as I seem to have forced the computer or the I-phone to do my bidding.

Weather

Our recent weather reminds me of our move to Atlanta, Georgia in the fall of 1973. I heard countless tales of "last winter's ice storm." There were travails of being without power, the trees were devastated, streets were impassable and life generally came to a halt. I suppose we have experienced the Texas version of that for the past several days. However, by the time you read this, I expect all the ice will have melted, trees will have resumed their shapes and we will be out of our cocoons. We will probably be talking about the ice storm of '07 for years to come.

Having lived in Milwaukee, Wisconsin, Washington, D.C., and Carlisle, Pennsylvania, I am not terribly intimidated by a spate of weather such as we have just endured. Nevertheless, I heeded the media admonitions and stayed home. As I am unemployed—unless you count writing this column as employment and that would be a stretch—I had no reason to leave the house.

Normally, I manage to get to the gym about three days a week and I try to ride my bike 25 to 30 miles two days a week. With the weather as an excuse, I could, without guilt, forgo those activities. My wife usually walks three to four miles a day and finds innumerable places to go in her spare time. Our days are reasonably full, despite our lack of gainful employment. So, this weather has thrown us together in ways that we are not accustomed. We had to find things to occupy our time.

First, we slept late. In our house that means we didn't get up until 7:00 a.m. I remember when I was up at five and in the PT formation by 7:00. I swore then, that I would sleep until noon when I retired.

By the time I retired, I couldn't comfortably sleep past 7:00. Age is a thief. It stole my dreams of always waking up in the daylight.

Second, we watched a lot more TV than we normally watch. Well, we watched TV until we became completely overwhelmed with the "all about the storm all the time" reporting. It was as if we were experiencing a 100-year-level catastrophe x 2. I was able to tolerate the endless, breathless, fearless reporting until they replaced *Jeopardy* with a weather report. OK, ignore the war in Iraq, the recovery of the kidnapped boys, cancel *Judge Judy*, but eliminate *Jeopardy*! NEVER!

So, I delved into a couple of books I have been nibbling on for the past month. I finished Bob Woodward's 500-page *State of Denial* and made significant inroads into David McCullough's *Truman* tome.

My wife, though reared in Pittsburgh, Pennsylvania, (there is a Pittsburgh in Texas, you know) began searching for something warming to occupy her. She was drawn to the kitchen. Nothing more warming to the body and the soul than a big pot of soup, right? First, it was black-bean soup. With cornbread. Truly, it did the trick. There was a sense of contentment and delight as we enjoyed our comfort food and sympathized with the road crews, the line crews, mail men and other public servants who are on-call around the clock in this type weather. The next day she made chicken soup and that abated the chill somewhat.

We made numerous trips to our computers to check our email. Surely, there are others whose travel is limited to their front sidewalk to retrieve the newspaper. They must be going to their computers as well. But they were not writing to us. Actually, I began to be excited when I had a message, even though it was spam for Viagra.

I googled esoteric words I normally ignore. Do you know what perfervid means? I didn't think so. It means overly fervent. A few more days of ice and I'll be writing like George Will...without the arrogance, I would hope.

We recognized the inherent trap that lay before us. While togetherness is a great thing, there is a point of diminishing returns. Each of us needs a certain amount of space. Ergo, we tried to maintain a reasonable distance, though cooped up inside the four walls. When email rendered nothing, I turned to Free Cell, a computer card game similar to solitaire. After about 300 games, my eyes couldn't distinguish an ace from a deuce. When my wife asked if I wanted her to iron my underwear, I knew she was beginning to break. It was finally getting to her.

Wednesday morning, before the melt began, she had reached her limit. As I was about half-way through my oatmeal, she looked at me and inquired, "Are you going to change your clothes today?" I hadn't given it a thought, but I got the message, which was, "I'm really tired of looking at you." The rest of the day, I gave her lots of room and changed my clothes. Thursday, as the melt was taking place, she was still near the point of disintegration and the sight of me was a trigger. I could not go into the kitchen for coffee without creating a mini-Vesuvius eruption.

When the roads cleared, she went to Wal-Mart. That signaled a better day. A trip to Wal-Mart makes us all happy to be home for awhile.

Wedding Reception

The wedding is only a part of the getting married process. Once the bride to be (B-T-B) and the mother of the bride (M-O-B) decide on the wedding gown, the M-O-B dress, the bridesmaids dresses, the church/chapel/hall in which the actual ceremony will take place, the music to be played or sung, the flowers for the church/chapel/hall, the bride's bouquet, the words for the ceremony—do couples still write their own vows, as they did in the 60's?—and the minister to officiate over these vows, the planning is about half finished.

Next is the RECEPTION! Oh, yes, the RECEPTION! First order of business is the place. Where is this gala to be held? The church social hall, The country club, The Sons of Hermann Hall, The Uhland Fire Station or Pete's Tavern and Dance Hall. Depending on the location, I have provided the uninitiated with a guide to what to expect at each location.

At the RECEPTION to be held in the church social hall, be prepared to gorge on finger sandwiches and homemade cookies. The punch will most likely be pineapple/orange/cranberry and the heaviest thing in it will be the ice. If you stay more than a half-hour, you are a relative of the bride or groom. Odds are heavy that the bride had to pay for the reception.

If the RECEPTION is at the country club, the bride's family is reasonably affluent and have probably lived in the community for a while. The bride's dad plays golf while her mother plays bridge or tennis or both. Two hundred people will be invited and the hors d'ouvres will be heavy. The drinks will be adult beverages of about any variety. However, there very well may be a cutoff time, and that means go home.

If the RECEPTION is at The Sons of Hermann Hall, you know the family's been in the area for several generations and most likely can trace its origin in Texas to the early or mid 1800's. There will be an oompah band and if you plan to dance, you better know how to polka and schottische. Refreshments will be wurst and beer and there will be no cutoff time. It's entirely possible the bride will be the last person standing—at 6:00 AM the morning after. And she will still be wearing her wedding gown.

If the RECEPTION is at the Uhland Fire Station, count on barbecue and col'beer—among these folks, col'beer is one word. There will be a local band, most likely western swing, doing George Strait and George Jones. Lots of big hats, big belt buckles and big hair. Better know how to do the Texas two step and the cotton-eyed joe if you plan to dance. You will get better parking if you have a pick-up, preferably with 4-wheel drive and a tool box that spans the width of the pick-up bed. Livestock would be an appropriate wedding gift.

If Pete's Tavern and Dance Hall is the site of the RECEPTION, you might reasonably conclude that this is not the first rodeo for the blissful couple. Quite likely, they selected Pete's because they met there while drowning their sorrows over a "he/she that done me wrong." There may be a house band, but plan to dance to the juke box and most likely, there will be a cash bar. Don't count out the possibility of special entertainment. It is highly possible that one of the nuptial pair may become involved in a physical confrontation with an ex-wife/husband/sweetheart.

I have a friend who did wedding cakes for years. Wonder if she has special insights into the protocol of that time-honored ceremony, the RECEPTION.

Grackles

I love most birds and marvel in delight
As I watch them in their wondrous flight
There is one though, for which I have no use
It is a species which we could easily afford to lose

The grackle is a bird made for hatin'
Its feathers and its heart are black as Satan
They have no song, no tune, not the grackle
It's a compliment to say its voice is a cackle

Their great swarms are a cacophony of awful chatter
Stay away for they also produce a sizable splatter
We are told to honor all living things under the sun
But, I have to wonder about this son-of-a-gun

So, when this rascal and his flock descend
That's when my patience and tolerance end
I suppose I should be more understanding and devout
But I think this is one bird we could do without.

Bottled Water

Where did the bottled water fad come from? Had you told me a few years ago you were going to start a bottled water company, I would have said, "Yeah, and I'm reviving the Pet Rock craze." I would have never imagined that people would pay $2.00 for a bottle of something they can get for free right from the kitchen faucet. But then, Barnum or Bailey or W.C. Fields or Alfred E. Newman once said, "No one ever lost money underestimating the wisdom of the American public."

I must admit when I was a kid—looong time ago—we had bottled water. The bottle was a Mason jar, wrapped in burlap. We filled it with water, wet the burlap to cool it, and took it to the field with us when we chopped cotton; or we put it on the tractor when we plowed. We also carried water with us when we traveled. It was in a canvas bag that hung from the radiator cap of the '36 Ford sedan. Air blowing on the canvas bag was supposed to cool the water, but I could never determine that it did.

Of course, that is not the kind of bottled water we see today. I'm talking about the likes of Aquafina, Dasani, or Evian. (*Evian* is, appropriately, *naïve* spelled backwards. Look it up.) There are actually hundreds of brands of bottled water out there. The only thing more ubiquitous than bottled water these days is the cell phone.

Some of these waters are supposed to be "purified." Some are "fortified." Some are from "mountain springs." Some are flavored (yuck). And some are "energized."

I Googled three brands, just to see what they really have that makes them special.

Aquafina is made by the Pepsi Cola company, and is "derived from a municipal source." That is, it comes from some city water supply, just like your tap water. It is treated with reverse osmosis to remove nearly all the natural minerals, and that gives it a light mellow taste.

Dasani is made by the Coca Cola company, and it also comes from some city's tap water. Like Aquafina, it goes through reverse osmosis to remove most of the natural minerals, but, unlike Aquafina, some of the minerals are added back to the water.

Evian, a French product, comes from a natural aquifer at Haute Savoie. It was discovered in 1789 by the Marquise de Lessert and Google reports "...there is really nothing exceptional in Evian's chemistry besides the strong level of Silica and low sodium content."

No matter where you look someone is carrying a bottle of water or swigging from one. As far as I know, we still have public water fountains in most locations—grocery stores, gymnasiums, doctor's offices, ad infinitum. I admit that I have read that most of us are under-hydrated most of the time. My former wife admonished me about drinking more water. She said I don't drink enough.

As with almost every other issue, there are two sides to that one. One health article tells me to drink eight 12-ounce glasses of water every day. The next one tells me to drink when I'm thirsty. I drink when I'm thirsty—from the kitchen faucet or the public water fountain. Maybe I would be healthier if I drank the eight glasses of water a day, but, if I did, at my age, I would probably spend most of my time in the bathroom.

As a cyclist, I actually drink lots of water. Almost all cyclists have some form of water supply on the bike. Those who can ride and chew gum at the same time usually have a couple of water bottles attached to the bike frame. Occasionally, they will reach down, get the bottle, tip their head back and take a long draw. I carry a Camelbak on my back with a tube through which I can siphon water without letting go of the handlebars. And I don't have to take my eyes off the road.

Oh, I have a water bottle on my bike. It contains CO_2 cartridges, sun screen, and a cleaning rag.

This is not a tirade against bottled water. I admit, we buy it from time to time, but I get a queasy feeling when we do. Not because Evian is naïve spelled backwards, but because the plastic bottles are a real nuisance. I understand they are filling the landfills and have a life span in excess of 900 years. Further, there are rumors that some of the plastic bottles contain unsafe chemicals that contaminate the water. That seems to make bottled water a lose/lose situation.

Nevertheless, wherever you go, there are people with that ever-present bottle of water. Makes me wonder if George Strait ever gets calls about that "…ocean-front property in Arizona."

The Segway Scooter

What is all the fuss about the Segway Scooter which was recently unveiled? Am I the only person in the world who did not know Dean Kamen was working on a device which was reputedly going to change the way we live? And what did we get? Quoting Tim McDonald of NewFactor Network, "After all the hype, speculation and just plain curiosity that have rippled through the high-tech world for nearly a year, it turns out that the top secret, world-changing, super-invention code named 'IT' is... a scooter."

Kamen is quoted as saying, "Cities need cars like fish need bicycles." While there may be a great deal of truth in that statement, getting people to give up cars has proven a major problem in most of the cities of this country. Our own neighbor, Austin, just 30 miles north on the linear parking lot known as IH 35, has a bus system which has offered citizens free transportation if they would leave their cars at home. Didn't work. I do not visualize this gadget filling the sidewalks of New York or replacing the taxi-cab. I certainly can not imagine those huge circular parking lots in Houston, San Antonio and Dallas, known respectively as Highway 610, 410 and 435, full of little electric scooters moving at the top speed of 17 miles an hour.

Kamen insists that 'IT' will replace cars as our favorite form of urban transportation. He says the Segway Human Transporter, a one-person, battery-powered, self-balancing scooter will revolutionize the way the world designs cities. Its financial backers say the company will be the fastest in history to reach a billion dollars in sales. While all this may come to pass, I am no more eager to invest in the future of this scooter than I was to spend $30,000.00 on a pair of emus.

265

The claim is that this is a technological marvel. It has 10 microprocessors, aviation grade gyroscopes, an accelerometer, a cluster of tilt sensors, two batteries and bundles of complex 'intuitive' computer software. It can travel approximately 15 miles on a charge of electricity costing about a dime. It sounds a bit like the old Rube Goldberg cartoons where he designed machines which required 16 operations to break an egg. Newsweek, in its Conventional Wisdom section, gives it a down arrow and says "Superhyped mystery invention is cool but pricey, impractical scooter."

Bicycles have been around for a hundred years or more. They are cheap, practical, reasonably safe and virtually unused in this country by anyone over 13 years old. The car is seen as a constitutional right by every kid when he/she reaches the 16th birthday. And a huge number of parents support that belief. So, if we are going to remove cars from the cities, we must launch a major education program to change attitudes. I can't help wondering how much better Kamen could have made the bicycle, had he spent the time, energy and money on that already quiet, non-polluting, energy efficient machine which has the added benefit of providing exercise for the user.

It seems to me what we have here is a device not much more useful than a yo yo and probably not as much fun. However, I can imagine some practical uses for it. For example, in a hospital with interminable hallways, one can imagine a couple of scooters located at the nurses' station. They would facilitate making rounds and, in the event of an emergency, might be an enhancement to a medical person arriving at the scene sooner. The Segway might very well be the answer to getting cops out of their cars and on a sidewalk beat. It is hyped as the first enhancement to personal mobility that doesn't isolate the user from other pedestrians.

In the next millennium population growth will likely make the automobile obsolete. There will then be a need for a machine similar to the Segway Human Transporter. It is refreshing to see someone is ahead of his time in developing such a device. But until it has a CD player with a stereo sound system, heating and AC, leather accouterments, power steering and cruise control, it will remain a novelty, and at $3,000.00 a pop, will be a curious toy for people with way too much money.

TV Reality Shows

I been thinkin' about TV reality shows. There are at least 20 on the air. Those I have seen are about as credible as Eva Gabor lecturing on quantum physics. TV reality shows are the pulp fiction of programming. No, that's an insult to pulp fiction. They illustrate the paucity of creativity in the industry and its willingness to pander to the lowest common denominator of the viewing public.

Turn it off if you don't like it, you say. I do that, but still question the effect these insipid concoctions have on the viewers, especially the young and impressionable kids who seem to put them in the category of video games. TV reality shows have reached a level of inanity which exceeds my understanding of entertainment.

TV reality shows take the mundane and try to make it dramatic and entertaining. I find them mind-numbing boring. They are anything but reality. Try to imagine, if you will, how much danger members of The Survivor face with a TV camera crew recording their every move. Boy Scout campouts present one with more spontaniety and danger than The Survivor. A high school cheer leading contest is a great deal more risky and interesting than all the stunts they concoct. The stunts are childish and have to be somewhat embarrassing to the participants who have a brain larger than a lima bean.

Shows like Big Brother and the Osbournes are literally the excrement of entertainment. One entire episode of the Osbournes deals with the discovery and disposition of dog poop. There are five or six dogs in the family and quite honestly, the dogs are more interesting than the people. I can't understand a word any of the Osbournes utters and I think I'm probably not missing a darn thing.

Big Brother takes us back to the fourth grade where we formed cliques for the sole purpose of excluding others. The participants swear allegiance to others for the duration of the show, knowing full well they are going to vote whichever way is most beneficial to themselves, regardless of their alliances. What's the message of a show such as this one? That loyalty and allegiance has no place in life; that losers are those who live up to their word. And if you are an effective influence in your community, someone will betray you to promote his/her own agenda. The only redeeming quality I can identify on this show is that it allows us to watch on TV someone as bored as we must be to watch this show.

What is the mindset of people who watch TV reality shows. Have our brains so thoroughly turned to mush that we are satisfied watching people in the daily doldrums of a really, really dull life or in situations so trite and contrived they don't measure up to the games we played as 10 year-olds.

A group of 10 year-olds playing tree tag is more suspenseful and exciting than all the reality shows I have seen. Watching construction from the sidewalk is absolutely ingtriguing compared to Fear Factor. Come to think of it, construction has been incoporated into a reality show. Two as a matter of fact–Trading Spaces and While You Were Gone. The interior designers show some creativity on each of these shows, however, people allow themselves to be pawns in the interest of 15 minutes of TV fame.   Joe Millionaire, a self-confessed phony premise, which turned out to be doubly phony, concluded recently. Twenty-five young women went before the TV cameras revealing their moral turpitude. I was reminded of the story of the man who approached a young lady at a cocktail party and asked if she would go to bed with him for $1 million. She immediately said she would. He then asked if she would do the same for $10. She huffily asked, "What do you think I am?" He responded, "We have established that, we are just haggling over the price."

The Batchelor and the Batchelorette may be the most contrived of all. The eye candy, enhanced by the soft porn and the idiocy of the participants is over the top and escapes any definition of entertainment.

It is amazing that this country has been dumbed down from I Love Lucy, Seinfeld, Cheers, St. Elsewhere, The Carol Burnette Show and The Honeymooners to these remakes of the Gong Show. In a recap episode of The Bachelor, Helene proved that the Yogi Berra school of English usage is not dead with, "He re-proposed all over again." The Bachelorette wrap up episode contained this gem, "We will live happily ever after, forever."

Chuck Barris may have been a hit man for the CIA, so in the interest of self-preservation, maybe I need to apologize to the Gong Show.

Bumper Stickers

Are bumper stickers more revealing than we ever imagined? Recently driving along IH (stands for It's Hell) 35, I observed a bumper sticker which read, "I Visited the Snake Farm". It was on the rear bumper of a little Honda, Mitsubishi, Toyota or Nagano automobile. I can't tell them apart, and the driver was doing about 80 miles per hour in a 70 mph zone. He was zigging in and zagging out of the traffic lanes. It occurred to me anyone who would visit the snake farm where he would obtain such a bumper sticker would have the mentality of a fence post. And with a 3000 pound missile which he is steering at 80 mph, he has the explosive potential of a SCUD and a whole lot greater accuracy. Do we really need these guys adding to the mayhem on our six-lane ribbons of doom?

Is there something in a bumper sticker that reveals a dark side of us? With the prevalence of road rage these days, I have begun to observe bumper stickers with a new perspective. What about, If You Are Close Enough To Read This, You Are Too Damn Close. Is that driver a claustrophobic paranoic, watching his rear view mirror, waiting for you to register recognition of his message before he blows your head off as you go around him on the right? You have to pass on the right because these drivers always use the fast lane to memorialize Jimmy Carter's 55 mph national speed limit.

The other version of that bumper sticker is, If You Can Read This, Thank A Teacher. I wonder if this driver is one of those underpaid, under appreciated, overworked, burned out high school English teachers who, after 26 years of dedicated service, was let go for sexual harassment when he commented to the assistant princiipal that he liked her black oxfords. This is his way of expressing his cynicism. Get too close to him and he is ready to run you off the road just because HE'S MAD AND HE ISN'T GOING TO TAKE IT ANYMORE!!

Then there is We Are Spending Our Children's Inheritance. That one appears on the rear of an RV as big as a railroad car. The size of the monster reminds me of a 747 rumbling down the runway, trying to get airborne, and it gets the same gas mileage as an Abrams M-60 Tank. That is intimidating, but when I think the person driving that thing has major issues with his own kids, I wonder what his mood might be if I slightly resemble the alcoholic son, or my wife's blond hair reminds him of his daughter who took her college tuition and moved to New Mexico to live in a commune with a man twice her age who said he was the messenger from Mars. What evil lurks in the minds of men? Do bumper stickers give us a clue?

It seems innocuous enough, but Native Texan really scares me. Should we be bragging about being enamored with the geographical and governmental entity that has: a) legally killed more people in the past 12 months than all the other 49 states combined; b) legalized carrying concealed weapons by the very people I am describing in the foregoing paragraphs; c) elected Ralph Nixon to the Texas State Senate; d) almost contracted to bury nuclear waste in one of the most pristine areas of the world; e) and has the distinction of being the LAST state in the union to allow its citizens to make home equity loans. Does that bumper sticker cause you to have second thoughts about what kind of jingoistic loyalties might underlie the purchase of same?

Then there is, I Wasn't Born In Texas But I Got Here As Soon As I Could. Unless the wearer of this one was born in Oklahoma, I certainly have to wonder about him/her. All of the comments pertaining to Native Texan apply and then I have to ask, Why? Was (s)he wanted for an axe murder? Did he rob a Savings and Loan? Seems you could do that legally in Texas when we had Savings and Loans. Is he avoiding child support? How many times has (s)he been married? Were there sufficient and timely divorces?

Another common bumper sticker is, If This Thing's Rockin', Don't Come A Knockin'. This one appears almost exclusively on RV's and if that is someone's idea of humor, I can not imagine knocking... ever...rocking, or otherwise. They are most assuredly safe from my interference.

When Guns Are Outlawed, Only Outlaws Will Have Guns is a sticker that really gets to me. The first assumption is (s)he will most assuredly have a gun in the glove compartment. Second, (s)he loves to use it and looks for any opportunity to do so. Consequently, I conclude I am following the proverbial loose cannon whose favorite actor is Charlton Heston and whose favorite of the Ten Commandments is "Thou shalt not commit murder.......without a good cause."

The next time you see a bumper sticker, ask yourself what is the person in that car trying to tell me about him/herself. Analyzing bumper stickers is more fun than counting fence posts or out of state licenses. Give yourself a break and avoid road hypnosis. Let your fellow travelers entertain...or frighten you.

Printed in the United States
By Bookmasters